The LearningWheel

Model of Digital Pedagogy

Deborah Kellsey & Amanda M L Taylor

Other books you may be interested in:

Digital Literacy for Primary Teachers
Moira Savage & Anthony Burnett
ISBN 978-1-909682-61-0

Social Media and Social Work Education
Edited by Joanne Westwood
ISBN 978-1-909682-57-3

Technology-enhanced Learning in the Early Years Foundation Stage
Moira Savage, Anthony Burnett & Michelle Rogers
ISBN 978-1-911106-18-0

Titles are also available in a range of electronic formats. To order please go to our website www.criticalpublishing.com or contact our distributor NBN International, 10 Thornbury Road, Plymouth PL6 7PP, telephone 01752 202301 or email orders@nbninternational.com

The
LearningWheel

A Model of Digital Pedagogy

Deborah Kellsey & Amanda M L Taylor

First published in 2017 by Critical Publishing Ltd

British Library Cataloguing in Publication Data
A CIP record for this book is available from the British Library

ISBN: 978-1-911106-38-8

This book is also available in the following e-book formats:
MOBI: 978-1-911106-39-5
EPUB: 978-1-911106-40-1
Adobe e-book reader: 978-1-911106-41-8

Cover design by Out of House
Project Management by Out of House Publishing
Printed and bound in Great Britain by

Critical Publishing
3 Connaught Road
St Albans
AL3 5RX

www.criticalpublishing.com

HELP US TO HELP YOU!

Our aim is to help you to become the best professional you can be. In order to improve your critical thinking skills we are pleased to offer you a **free booklet** on the subject.

Just go to our website www.criticalpublishing.com and click the Free Resources link on the home page. The booklet is in the Study Skills section.

We have more free resources on our website which you may also find useful.

If you'd like to write a review of this book on Amazon, Books Etc or Wordery, **we would be happy to send you the digital version of the book for free.**

Email a link to your review to us at admin@criticalpublishing.com, and we'll reply with a PDF of the book, which you can read on your phone, tablet or Kindle.

You can also connect with us on:

Twitter@CriticalPub #criticalpublishing

Facebook www.facebook.com/Critical-Publishing-456875584333404

Our blog https://thecriticalblog.wordpress.com

CONTENTS

LIST OF ILLUSTRATIONS

MEET THE **AUTHORS**

DEBORAH KELLSEY is the Director for Digital & IT Services at a further education college, where she is responsible for driving technology-enhanced learning and embedding technology within staff and student practice. With over 20 years' teaching experience in both further and higher education in visual communication and as a practising graphic designer, Deborah has forged successful collaborations with internal, external and international stakeholders. Deborah is passionate about learning technologies and is eager to connect with others involved in education, technology and the creative industries. Her excellent proven track record for creative thinking, sharing best practice and knowledge exchange is optimised in the LearningWheel tool found here: http://learningwheel.co.uk/. This is a resource she developed to help bridge the gap between traditional teaching methods and contemporary digital learning content and resources.

In 2016 Deborah was named in the JISC Top 50 further education influencers on social media.

@DebKellsey

@LearningWheel #LearningWheel

AMANDA M L TAYLOR is currently employed as a senior lecturer in the School of Social Work at the University of Central Lancashire. Before her academic career, Amanda was a psychiatric social worker in Northern Ireland, specialising in community mental health and services for people whose first language is signed communication. However, it was Amanda's interest in the development of creative teaching methodologies, ones that can engage students in a dynamic, meaningful and informative manner, that brought her to England and to social work education. She is known for her work in the area of technologies in social work education, evidenced through her internationally renowned innovation 'The Use of Book Groups in Social Work Education and Practice'. This is a teaching and learning methodology that can be found on Twitter: @ SWBookGroup and on Storify: https://storify.com/AMLTaylor66/ the-use-of-book-clubs-in-social-work-education.

Amanda's current research considers the contribution of social work education to the digital socialisation of student social workers throughout their professional training, in preparation for practice.

In 2015 Amanda was named in the JISC top 50 higher education influencers on social media.

@amltaylor66

@SWBookGroup #swbk

FOREWORD

There has been much written about the use of technology as a means of enhancing the way we live, learn and teach. However, the exponential growth of technology has meant that aside from the early adopters, it can still be both daunting and difficult to keep abreast of what seem like innovative and exciting new approaches to learning and teaching. Furthermore, understanding what innovations to choose to enhance the learning experience can be clouded by the desire to grasp the new and the shiny. A typical example is the iPad. Once through the hoops of purchasing the equipment, the teacher celebrates the acquisition of 30–40 shiny tablets and can often then be left thinking, 'Ah so what will I get my student to do on Monday using the iPads?...'

In order to help educators to develop their practice, it is vital that they are introduced to the many ways other educators are already embracing, which enable them to *connect* and *communicate* in order to share the new, innovative and often pioneering ways they are enhancing their own curricula. They need to learn how to *curate* resources and approaches, and in time build confidence to *collaborate* with others to adapt or *create* further new resources. Becoming aware of the ways the 5Cs (Nerantzi and Beckingham, 2015) can enhance both their own practice and that of others is the first step. Adopting the ethos of global sharing, where all educators can benefit, providing numerous opportunities to form supportive networks to explore further innovations in the future is the next step.

The LearningWheel offers a firm foundation for this step change in practice to be realised. This book introduces a solid framework that has been tried and tested by educators from a multitude of disciplines and within a range of educational settings, including further education and higher education. The LearningWheel is a sound model of digital pedagogy that is both accessible and inclusive. It steers us away from succumbing to the technology driving the learning to examples that will guide the reader to engage in the communication, collaboration, learning content and assessment, which will enhance the learning and teaching experience.

The book is essential reading for teachers, educational developers, learning technologists, trainers, support staff, as well as senior management looking to develop their institutional digital strategy. It provides the reader with information about the framework and brings this to life with a wide range of case studies to demonstrate its application. The authors guide the reader to focus on how as educators they may enhance and facilitate new approaches that will have a positive impact on the learning experience of the students they are teaching. The LearningWheel quite clearly integrates both research and practice and as such provides readers with a valuable resource that they will refer back to again and again, both for their own practice and pedagogical research. It is a must for the bookshelf of every 21st-century educator. It will certainly become a well-thumbed edition taking pride of place on my own bookshelf.

Sue Beckingham (@suebecks).
Senior Lecturer in Information Systems, Educational Developer in Technology Enhanced Learning, and Senior Fellow of the Higher Education Academy.
Sheffield Hallam University

ACKNOWLEDGEMENTS

The inaugural Social Media for Learning in Higher Education Conference was held on 18 December 2015 at Sheffield Hallam University. We attended as a result of having papers accepted: Deborah's paper was 'The LearningWheel' outlining this digital pedagogical approach as a means to engaging learners through digital technologies and Amanda's seminar 'When Actual Met Virtual' provided an overview of how through connecting online the 'Use of Book Groups in Social Work Education' became an international Community of Learning. Before the conference and indeed throughout the conference we had not formally met; in fact, it was on the eve of the event that we virtually connected on the social media platform Twitter through the use of the conference hashtag #SocMedHE15. However, a serendipitous mix-up in train journeys resulted in a very interesting conversation from which the idea for this book was born.

We would like to thank each and every one of the students and colleagues who have tolerated our innovative and driven natures and engaged with us as we have tried out our ideas. More particularly, we would like to offer a special thank you to all of those who have contributed to the LearningWheel and embraced this teaching and learning methodology wholeheartedly. Our collective ideas and efforts as a Virtual Community of Learning and Practice can only but improve and enrich the overall student experience.

On a more personal note …

I would like to express my gratitude to the then stranger on the train (Amanda), who offered and has delivered on her promise to write about the LearningWheel. Sacrificing endless hours, days, weeks and months, Amanda has literally interrogated the enthusiastic ideas of my mind to enable her to articulate in such an interesting manner the What? Why? and How? of the LearningWheel concept. She entered into the collaborative spirit of the LearningWheel to develop and refine what has become a shared labour of love! Thank you Amanda.

I would also like to acknowledge my daughter Kellsey by reminding her to 'learn from yesterday, live for today and hope for tomorrow … the important thing is not to stop questioning' (Einstein).

D Kellsey

And,

I would like to take this opportunity to thank Deborah for running with the suggestion to write about the LearningWheel. For trusting me to interpret this visually strong digital model accurately, and for affording me the honour of articulating the LearningWheel methodology through the writing of this book. I can only hope that I have done it justice. In addition, I offer thanks to the colleagues from my community of practice who have provided critical friendship throughout the writing of this book. Ali Gardner, Dr Denise Turner and Dr Jadwiga Leigh your time, belief and encouragement has been invaluable. Finally, I would like to acknowledge my son Ben for his ongoing support of my academic endeavours.

A M L Taylor

GLOSSARY

Assessment:	*the process of evaluating someone or something*
Asynchronous Communication:	*not requiring a response at that moment*
Blended Learning:	*employing physical and virtual teaching methods simultaneously as a learning activity*
BYOD:	*bring your own device, a term used for encouraging learners to bring their own mobile devices into learning spaces to promote and support engagement*
Communication:	*the process of transmitting, imparting or exchanging information, and views through verbal, non-verbal written and digital mediums*
Community of Practice (CoP):	*a collective of professionals who come together to develop ideas and work on a project*
Community of Learning (CoL):	*a collective of learners that come together to create knowledge, engage in learning activities and to learn together*
Computer-mediated Communication:	*communication facilitated by computers*
Collaboration:	*working together with another or in a group for the purpose of utilising collective knowledge, skills and effort to produce something.*
Crowd-sourced:	*generating content from individuals through social media networks*
Digital Literacy:	*the ability to find, evaluate, utilise, share, and create content using digital resources, information technologies and the internet*
Engagement:	*the degree of attention, curiosity and motivation that learners demonstrate when they are learning or being taught*
Learning Content:	*curriculum content that is collated and shared to generate learning. Resources and information made available in physical or digital formats. This could be a book, a website or a digital platform*
Pedagogy:	*the method and practice of teaching*

Spokes:

concise suggestions offered by teachers for teachers – that outline the digital resources being used to establish and support learning

**Technology-enhanced
Learning (TEL):**

the use of technology to support and maximise learning

**Virtual Community of Learning
and Practice (VCoL&P):**

a community of learners or practitioners who communicate and engage in online spaces for a common purpose

**Virtual Learning
Environment (VLE):**

a learning environment which is hosted on a web based platform within a education context. Sometimes referred to as Computer Learning Systems (CLS) or Virtual Learning Space (VLS). These spaces are multifunctional in design and aim to support teaching and learning activities

Why the LearningWheel?

As Laurillard (2007) explains:

in teaching and learning currently, we tend to use technology to support traditional modes of teaching – improving the quality of lecture presentations using interactive whiteboards, making lecture notes readable in PowerPoint and available online, extending the library by providing access to digital resources and libraries, recreating face-to-face tutorial discussions asynchronously online – all of them good, incremental improvements in quality and flexibility, but nowhere near being transformational.

(Laurillard, 2007, cited in Beetham and Sharpe, 2013, p xv)

We are not professing to be 'transformational' but we will claim to be aspirational, in that we believe the LearningWheel to have transformative potential, particularly given its collective and collaborative nature.

So why are we writing about the LearningWheel? Firstly, we are writing about it due to how well it has been received in practice and secondly to draw further attention to the use of digital technologies in education – those that can support, secure and, where relevant, transform teaching practices. More particularly, we write to those educators who are experiencing, in a very real sense, the influence of technologies on the learning landscape, and for whom the use of trending technologies in education is relatively new. It is this audience that we most hope to reach, as we remember back to when we each took the leap and embraced the digital age in its fullest. At that time we respectively sought practice examples and sources of support but there was little in the way of theoretical or practical advice readily available, usage was disparate and was often technology as opposed to pedagogy led. Our immediate communities of practice appeared split into users and non-users, believers and non-believers. We were unconvinced by the either-or arguments and felt that there was a middle ground that we needed to explore and a group of like-minded colleagues that we needed to find. The development of the LearningWheel model reflects these struggles and what we each sought. From its modest beginnings it has grown into a Virtual Community of Learning and Practice (VCoL&P) with contributors situated in a number of continents across the world. It is our hope that as you peruse the pages of this book that you too will see its value and take up your place in this growing global education network. We begin this book by setting into context the way in which we perceive digitisation to be influencing and shaping the educational landscape. The reflections offered are based upon our collective experiences as educators within further and higher education and the changes that we have encountered in our pursuit of excellence in teaching and learning.

There can be little doubt that technological advancements are gaining momentum, and it is our belief that if we as educators do not embrace the connected age, those we are educating will not be equipped to function within the digital societies in which their futures lie. Indeed, a premise on which all our futures, to a degree, rely. Relevant therefore are the findings of a recent UK government study that reported *'some 72% of employers state that they are unwilling to interview candidates who do not have basic IT skills'* (Blackwood, 2016, p 7). Inasmuch as the term 'basic' is unhelpfully vague and difficult to quantify, the statistics offered provide perspective on both the scale and type of problem that could arise if matters pertaining to digital literacy are not confronted. Employability issues such as this link directly to education, where the use of technologies remains the subject of much debate. It goes without saying that digital pedagogy, like most things in the education context, is a fluid and emerging concept. It is one that we believe deserves to be put much higher on the agenda, and part of this is the timely re-evaluation of teaching practices across a range of settings; be that primary, secondary, further, higher and even commercial education. It is hardly surprising, given the impact of technologies on the world at large, that educators are being challenged to refashion their methods. Each of us, in our respective roles, see and 'feel' this challenge first hand, on what seems like a daily basis. We refer throughout this book to an emergent body of literature, written by like-minded colleagues who are, and have been, providing not only evidence of the need for technology-related change within the teaching profession, but also providing access to said change through the development of resources aimed at bridging digital knowledge gaps.

In addition, and in an attempt to locate the need for this book further, we draw on the work of Susskind and Susskind (2015). We make reference to their most recent publication, *The Future of the Professions: How Technology will Transform the Work of Human Experts* (Susskind and Susskind, 2015) because of how it has influenced and shaped our thinking throughout the writing of this book. Their work outlines how a number of professions are being forced to reconceptualise their purpose due to the way in which technologies are forging unprecedented change to professional practices. Inasmuch as their work does not have a sole education focus, they do make comment on the future of education. They use the term *'post-professional society'* (p 105) to frame the near future, authenticating this conjecture with examples of change from within a number of professions; occurrences that are frankly quite staggering. In one such account they describe the successful removal of *'a gall bladder ... [from] a woman in France'* while the surgical team, assisted by robots, remained in the US (Susskind and Susskind, 2015, p 50). There are many other accounts, each of which demonstrate how technologies are reshaping traditional practices and in essence the characteristics of professional groupings. Additionally, and with direct reference to teaching, they remind us of the work of King, who alerted educators to the way in which the *'guide on the side'* was replacing the *'sage on the stage'* (1993, p 30). The Susskinds, however, accurately align this current, very real and seismic shift in the teacher role with the access to knowledge that technology now affords (2015, p 60). In direct correlation they cite statistics that show that *'more people signed up for Harvard's MOOCs in a single year than have attended the university in its 377 years' existence'* (Susskind and Susskind, 2015, p 58).

For us the Susskinds' work re-emphasises the rapidity and magnitude of change associated with digital developments, and again brings into sharp focus what we as educators already know: that like all other professions, teaching is not exempt from the impact of technology. These are insights that should in effect lead us to choose pragmatism over inertia, because as they conclude:

inaction, as well as action is a choice. [and] if we choose to do nothing, and ... default to our traditional ways and discard the promise of technological change for fear, say, of rocking the boat, then this is a decision for which the later generations can hold us responsible.

(Susskind and Susskind, 2015, p 307)

This is a sobering thought that serves as a reminder of the need for the re-evaluation of teaching practices so as to ensure that they are in keeping with the needs of learners in the connected age. As educators with a vested interest in digitisation we have found that there remains an inconsistent, and at times polarised, response to technologies across the profession. On the one hand they are viewed as helpful, enabling and non-threatening, and on the other troublesome, disruptive and hindering; with those in the middle feeling othered as they fit into neither camp. We have, however, visionary academics such as Laurillard (2008) to thank for remaining optimistic and more importantly realistic about digitisation. Even in her recognition that *'technology is forcing the pace of change'*, her discourse is energising, as she goes on to discuss the, *'intriguing potential ways ... [that technologies could contribute] to the adaptability of the sector, in its response to change'* (p 532). Loveless's (2011) work builds pragmatically upon Laurillard's optimism, driving her to call for educators to review their use of technologies in education, *'in the light of ... developments in understandings of pedagogy'* (p 301). Encouraging here is the appreciation, not only of the possibilities made available through engagement with technologies to develop teaching practices, but also the realism within which it is framed.

In spite of the fact that there is an increasing acknowledgement across the sector in terms of the demands and possibilities of digitisation, the question in our minds is how much has changed in the period of time that has passed? There are notable time lags throughout the literature, which prompt us to question the cohesion between technological advancement and technology usage in practice. If we assume that Lightbody (2015, p ix) is correct in his more recent assertion that *'pedagogy needs to rapidly shift ... because we are already falling behind the curve'*, then he confirms what our educational experiences tell us; that there remains much to do. Although, realistically this will always be the case, given that to some degree the *'curve'* will invariably remain out of reach.

So perhaps the most viable way forward is that previously suggested by Loveless (2011), who asserts the need for a proactive approach to the evaluation of digital literacy in education that is grounded in the emerging pedagogy; all of which she accurately aligns with the requirements for *'continuing professional development'* (CPD) (p 312). It is this type of ideology that is evident in the tenacious and tireless work of colleagues such as Davis et al (2015) from the Joint Information Systems Committee (JISC), who offer a *'model ... [through which teachers can] define the[ir] digital capabilities'* (p 1). This is work which demonstrates that the digital development of educators is, for some, firmly on the agenda and as a result mediums to facilitate progression are being made available. This work is crucial to the progression of teaching methodologies and the currency of education in the digital age, because at no other time has it been more important to think about how learners are being prepared to take up their place in what has become a global workplace. Education and employment can no longer be thought about in 'local' terms and educators have a role to play. However, this is not straightforward, and as Susskind and Susskind (2015, p 105) state, *'educators are unsure what they are training the next generation of professionals to become'*. Even more relevant is the fact that not all educators have been professionally socialised using 21st-century technologies (Koehler and Mishra, 2009); therefore, it is safe to assume that knowledge gaps exist. Indeed, the more recent work of Kivunja (2013) examining the training of pre-service teachers concluded that *'it is incumbent upon ... education providers, to ensure that graduates are well prepared to be effective teachers for the digital generation'* (p 131), evidencing that digital deficits persist. Consequently, the changes necessary should be considered systematically; in that further attention needs to be paid to all of the stakeholders in the educational milieu, including the environment itself. In this way the educator, the learner, the learning content and the teaching context are seen as integral to the cohesion of the learning process. We believe that the LearningWheel model being presented here is one example of a workable solution.

What is the LearningWheel?

The swathe of innovative practice (Learning Futures, 2015) being shared through social media networks such as Twitter is reassuring. It was as a result of Deborah's role as the head of e-learning within a further education setting that led to the LearningWheel innovation coming to fruition. Central to this role was the dissemination of an e-learning strategy that was driven by a digital shift in education (HEFCE, 2009) at that time. An appraisal of the professional development of educators alongside the pace of technological innovations led to the careful screening of a range of digital tools to ascertain those most suitable for progressing practice in a contemporary teaching context. Key to this screening was the notion of collaboration, which was to be realised through the nurturing of *'learning communities'* (Wenger, 2000, p 215). Thus, the *'LearningWheel'* (Kellsey, 2013), a model of digital pedagogy, was born. The LearningWheel (Figure i) is informed by both technology-enhanced learning and blended learning methodologies. The former is explained by Walker et al (2014, p 4) as *'any online facility or system that directly supports learning and teaching'*, with the latter being described by Graham (2006, cited in Yuping et al, 2015, p 380) as the fusion of *'face-to-face instruction and computer-mediated instruction'*.

THE LEARNINGWHEEL
A model of digital pedagogy

www.learningwheel.co.uk

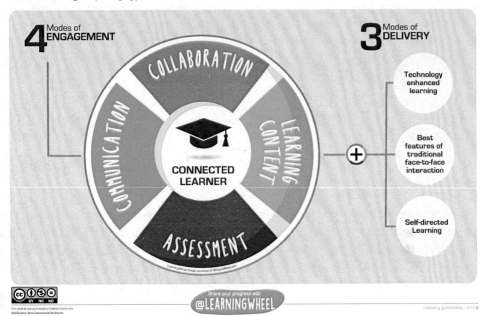

Figure i LearningWheel: A model of digital pedagogy.

The LearningWheel: A model of digital pedagogy http://learningwheel.co.uk/about-the-learning-wheel/model-digital-pedagogy/ (Kellsey, 2013).

It was initially developed as a language tool aimed at aligning traditional teaching methods and content with unfamiliar contemporary digital applications and resources. Through its functionality it was further developed into an evaluative model designed to enable educators to connect the old with the new, in an attempt to highlight and promote the core of that which is *'blended learning'* (Loh et al, 2016, p 133). Its design and purpose stem from and build upon the important and timely work of Sharpe et al (2006), whose *'pedagogic framework for e-learning'* offered *'modes of engagement'* (p 5) as a means to consider digital content and processes in an attempt to develop digital practices that would impact positively upon the student experience (Figure ii).

Mode 1
baseline course administration and learner support
Use web to distribute course information and carry out course administration (chosen from the following): aims and objectives, assessment criteria/proformas, past exam questions and model answers/assessment sheets, timetabling announcements, reading lists, tutor contact details, course evaluation tools, FAQs, additional web resources, links to field level resources, course/module handbook, lecture notes.

Mode 2	
blended learning leading to significant enhancements to learning and teaching processes	
Communication	**Assessment**
Provide improved tutor–student, student–student communications, mainly using discussion boards or email. Enable students, especially in disparate groupings and locations, to exchange information, ask questions and discuss issues relating to the course.	Provide improved feedback to students on their learning via computer assisted assessment for either formative (self-assessment and monitoring of progress) or summative (examination and grading) purposes or both. May involve electronic setting, submission and return of student assignments using digital artefacts and proformas where objective testing inappropriate.
Collaboration	**Learning content**
Provide a platform for collaborative student projects, involving shared responsibility for resources and outcomes. Students use communication tools and shared directory to collaborate on task processes and outcomes.	Develop flexible access to high quality, reusable learning content, which may include structured gateways to web and other resources with accompanying self-paced independent learning activities, interactive tutorials with feedback, simulations, study and learning skills resources and activities fostering independent learning.

Mode 3
online course/module
Develop module/course incorporating all or most of the above that can be delivered flexibly to allow learners to learn at times and places of their choosing. Likely to include presentation of course materials, communication between tutor and students, self-assessment and monitoring of progress.

Figure ii Modes of engagement (Sharpe et al, 2006, p 6).

Visual and interactive dimensions were added (Figure i) to provide educators with a context in which they could proactively analyse and evaluate teaching content and delivery for practice in contemporary educational settings, the focus being an opportunity to engage with emerging technologies and to become familiar with the latest digital pedagogy. Significant is the way in which the LearningWheel facilitates the opportunity to build confidence, for educators and learners, pertaining to digital technologies through the application of those technologies across the range of curriculum areas. Not only does the LearningWheel provide an opportunity to engage with technologies that can enhance content and delivery, but it also functions as a means to scaffold assessment; which in turn increases the likelihood of improved academic outcomes (Garrison and Vaughan, 2008).

Each individual LearningWheel has a number of curated spokes that signpost teachers towards digital resources that have the potential to further engage learners in the following four modes: Learning Content, Communication, Collaboration, Assessment (Figure i). The model acknowledges the significance of learner engagement across all four modes, while recognising that some digital tools and resources can work effectively across multiple modes. It prompts educators to assess what learners already know about the digital world, and provides insights into how they might already collaborate in social networks online. The content of the LearningWheel is crowd-sourced via an asynchronous platform, with contributions sought from a range of individuals in both educational and technological settings across the globe. The result is a rich and relevant resource created by teachers for teachers. It is a model that can be used to inform, scaffold and compliment lesson planning and delivery through the application of technologies that have the potential to enhance teaching and learning; ones that can be built upon, collated and widely shared. Alongside all of this, it provides educators with a context in which to consider professional development in relation to the knowledge and skills required for practice within contemporary education (Carpenter and Krutka, 2015) in a digital respect. In totality, the LearningWheel is a space in which to explore what Loh et al (2016, p 130) describe as *'the intricate relationship between the need to use new e-learning technologies for educational purposes and the capability of its adoption to drive change in the way students want to and are willing to, learn'*.

Who is the LearningWheel for?

The LearningWheel was primarily designed to encourage educators with varying degrees of digital literacy and presence to consider contemporary teaching practices and to support them to develop further as futuristic practitioners, or as Verhaart (2012, p 191) prefers to call them, *'networked teacher[s]'*. It is a model that supports student-centric teaching and learning (Rahimi et al, 2015), validating the move away from the *'"I speak and you listen" pedagogy'* (Lightbody, 2015, p 1) for practice within the connected age. It prioritises *'learner empowerment'* (Ryan and Tilbury, 2013, p 5) and partnership and sees the teacher adopt what Susskind and Susskind (2015, p 60) refer to as the role of *'content curator'*. This is not to negate the fact that educators have always curated learning content, but to recognise that the nature of curation made available through technological advancement can result in a very different type of content and delivery. It is seamless the way in which it enables teachers to blend content, delivery and process. Furthermore, it adds to the body of educational methodologies that crucially situate learners firmly at the centre of the learning process with the aim of promoting deeper learning, which in essence should, as previously mentioned, lead to academic achievement. It does not support the view of online and offline as polarised positions in that it is 'blended' in nature, drawing on both face-to-face and online methodologies. As such, it *responds to the need for forms of pedagogic innovation that help to develop flexibility as an attribute or capability, in both learners and educators'* (Ryan and Tilbury, 2013, p 4), while affording educators with the opportunity to *'shape the discourse and be fully engaged'* (Garrison and Vaughan, 2008, p 26). The LearningWheel model is available to anyone involved in education and it is our hope that this model, or the ideas underpinning it, will become embedded not only into current teaching practices but also more significantly into Initial Teacher Training as a means to promoting technology-enhanced teaching and blended learning in a manner that reflects contemporary education. This in itself would help to avoid the potential pitfalls of viewing traditional and online methods as separate or unconnected.

CRITICAL **REFLECTION**

It would be useful at this point to pause and think through …

- *which digital tools are you currently using in your teaching practice?*
- *how are technologies impacting upon your teaching practice?*
- *what digital learning needs have you identified in relation to your professional development?*

You might find the work of White (2014) useful as you complete this reflective exercise. Various examples of the digital mapping tool that will assist you to develop your own can be found at the link below.

Example visitor and residents maps www.jisc.ac.uk/guides/evaluating-digital-services/example-visitor-and-resident-maps (White, 2014)

While we do not feel it necessary to get into an in-depth analysis of the merits of each of the methodological approaches that underpin the use of digital technologies in teaching and learning in this book, we would urge readers interested in these matters to pursue the fascinating critiques offered by both Oliver and Trigwell (2005) and Kirkwood and Price (2014). Furthermore, for an incredibly well constructed and pedagogically sound overview of emerging digital methodologies, the work of Mayes and de Freitas (2013) 'Technology-Enhanced Learning' and Sharpe and Oliver's (2013) 'Designing For Learning in Course Teams', both in Beetham and Sharpe's (2013) brilliant text, *Rethinking Pedagogy for a Digital Age*, are all useful starting points for developing one's thinking.

In the following four chapters, we weave our discussion around the rationale and pedagogy that underpins each of the modes of engagement that make up the LearningWheel and offer this knowledge as interactively as possible to enable readers to experientially engage with the text as an example of the emerging learning landscape. We provide visual representations taken from the LearningWheel website to illustrate the methods used to collate, communicate and share resources in each of the four modes of engagement. Woven into the text is the opportunity to contribute to a LearningWheel that will be uniquely crafted by readers of this book. Each contributor will be cited for the suggestion they offer on the website *The LearningWheel* http://learningwheel.co.uk/ (Kellsey, 2016).

In the conclusion we draw together the journey of the LearningWheel thus far and how through its development the sharing of practice that supports technology-enabled teaching and learning has been made possible. We would like to point out, however, that the LearningWheel is an emerging methodology; there have been many significant changes to the concept even since we began this book. We believe this is the beauty of technology-enhanced teaching and learning, in that it is a fluid concept that brings many advantages due to the way in which it can facilitate and nurture teacher and learner creativity. We would also like to note that in no way do we claim to be experts in the field, but we do feel that we have a contribution to make as we navigate new ways of being as contemporary educators. It is in this vein that we proceed.

REFERENCES

Beetham, H and Sharpe, R (2013) *Rethinking Pedagogy for a Digital Age: Designing and Delivering E-Learning*. New York: Routledge.

Blackwood, N (2016) Digital skills crisis: Second report of Session 2016–17. Report, together with formal minutes relating to the report ordered by the House of Commons. [online] Available at: http://dera.ioe.ac.uk/26605/1/270.pdf (accessed 24 June 2016).

Carpenter, J P and Krutka, D G (2015) Engagement through Microblogging: Educator Professional Development via Twitter. *Professional Development in Education*, 41(4): 707–28.

Davis, S, Clay, J and Phipps, L (2015) Building digital capability: Example teacher profile. [online] Available at: http://repository.jisc.ac.uk/6240/1/Digital_capabilities_teacher_profile.pdf (accessed 8 June 2016).

Garrison, D R and Vaughan, N D (2008) *Blended Learning in Higher Education: Framework, Principles and Guidelines*. San Francisco, CA: Jossey-Bass.

Graham, C R (2006) Blended Learning Systems: Definition, Current Trends, and Future Directions, in Bonk, C J and Graham, C R (eds) *Handbook of Blended Learning: Global Perspectives, Local Designs*, pp 3–21. San Francisco, CA: Pfeiffer Publishing.

HEFCE (2009) Enhancing Learning and Teaching through the Use of Technology: A Revised Approach to HEFCE's Strategy for E-Learning. [online] Available at: http://webarchive.nationalarchives.gov.uk/20100202100434/http://www.hefce.ac.uk/media/hefce1/pubs/hefce/2009/0912/09_12.pdf (accessed 27 March 2016).

Kellsey, D (2013) LearningWheel: A model of digital pedagogy. [online] Available at: http://learningwheel.co.uk/about-the-learning-wheel/model-digital-pedagogy/ (accessed 14 June 2016).

Kellsey, D (2016) The LearningWheel [website]. [online] Available at: http://learningwheel.co.uk/ (accessed 28 March 2016).

King, A (1993) From Sage on the Stage to Guide on the Side. *College Teaching*, 4(1): 30–35.

Kirkwood, A and Price, L (2014) Technology-Enhanced Learning and Teaching in Higher Education: What is 'Enhanced' and How Do We Know? A Critical Literature Review. *Learning, Media and Technology*, 39(1): 6–36.

Kivunja, C (2013) Embedding Digital Pedagogy in Pre-Service Higher Education to Better Prepare Teachers for the Digital Generation. *International Journal of Higher Education*, 2(4): 131–42.

Koehler, M and Mishra, P (2009) What is Technological Pedagogical Content Knowledge (TPACK)? *Contemporary Issues in Technology and Teacher Education*, 9(1): 60–70.

Laurillard, D (2007) Preface, in Beetham, H and Sharpe, R (2013) (eds) *Rethinking Pedagogy for a Digital Age: Designing and Delivering E-Learning*, pp xc–xvii. London: Routledge.

Laurillard, D (2008) Technology Enhanced Learning as a Tool for Pedagogical Innovation. *Journal of Philosophy of Education*, 42: 521–33.

Learning Futures (2015) Inspiring learning through technology. [online] Available at: http://lfutures.co.uk/learning-futures (accessed 25 April 2016).

Lightbody, B (2015) *The i-Learning Revolution: A New Pedagogy*. Batley: Collegenet Publications Limited.

Loh, C, Wong, D H, Quazi, A and Kingshott, R P (2016) Re-examining Students' Perception of E-Learning: An Australian Perspective. *International Journal of Educational Management*, 30(1): 129–39.

Loveless, A (2011) Technology, Pedagogy and Education: Reflections on the Accomplishment of What Teachers Know, Do and Believe in a Digital Age. *Technology, Pedagogy and Education*, 20(3): 301–16.

Mayes, T and de Freitas, S (2013) Technology-Enhanced Learning, in Beetham, H and Sharpe, R (eds) *Rethinking Pedagogy for a Digital Age: Designing and Delivering E-Learning*, pp 13–25. London: Routledge.

Oliver, M and Trigwell, K (2005) Can 'Blended' Learning Be Redeemed? *E-Learning and Digital Media*, 2(1): 17–26.

Rahimi, E, Berg, J and Veen, W (2015) A Learning Model for Enhancing the Student's Control in Educational Process using Web 2.0 Personal Learning Environments. *British Journal of Educational Technology*, 46(4): 780–92.

Ryan, A and Tilbury, D (2013) *Flexible Pedagogies: New Pedagogical Ideas*. York: Higher Education Academy.

Sharpe, R and Oliver, M (2013) Designing for Learning in Course Teams, in Beetham, H and Sharpe, R *Rethinking Pedagogy for a Digital Age: Designing and Delivering E-Learning*, pp 41–51. London: Routledge.

Sharpe, R, Benfield, G and Francis, R (2006) Implementing a University E-Learning Strategy: Levers for Change within Academic Schools. *ALT-J*, 14(2): 135–51. doi: 10.1080/09687760600668503.

Susskind, R E and Susskind, D (2015) *The Future of the Professions: How Technology Will Transform the Work of Human Experts*. Oxford: Open University Press.

Verhaart, M (2012) Curating Digital Content in Teaching and Learning using Wiki Technology. *Proceedings of the 12th IEEE International Conference on Advanced Learning Technologies, ICALT*, pp 191–93.

Walker, R, Voce, J, Nicholls, J, Swift, E, Ahmed, J, Horrigan, S and Vincent, P (2014) 2014 survey of technology enhanced learning for higher education in the UK. [online] Available at: www.ucisa.ac.uk/~/media/groups/dsdg/Tel%202014%20Final%2018%20August.ashx (accessed 20 May 2016).

Wenger, E (2000) *Communities of Practice: Learning, Meaning, and Identity*. Cambridge: Cambridge University Press.

White, D (2014) Example visitor and resident maps. *JISC: Evaluating Digital Services*. [online] Available at: www.jisc.ac.uk/guides/evaluating-digital-services/example-visitor-and-resident-maps (accessed 7 June 2016).

Yuping, W, Xibin, H and Juan, Y (2015) Revisiting the Blended Learning Literature: Using a Complex Adaptive Systems Framework. *Journal of Educational Technology & Society*, 18(2): 380–93.

Contextualising the need for content reform

We begin this first chapter by restating our acknowledgement of the rapidity of technological change characteristic of the connected age, while keeping sight of the value of innovation and blended learning and the affordances that each brings. Despite the fact that the connected age has, to some degree, changed the form and shelf-life of learning content and delivery (Lambert, 2014), each remains the cornerstone of and gateway to knowledge acquisition. Educators have consistently engaged with reform, be that policy driven, organisationally driven, or even changes to practices initiated by teachers themselves. However, there appears to be faster, more urgent and externally driven pressures to reform (BIS, 2015), and as such an increased danger for the construction of learning spaces that could reduce, as opposed to maximise, the potential for targeted and *personalised learning* (Buckingham, 2007, p 1943; McLoughlin and Lee, 2010, p 28). The UK government is moving swiftly on with its *'digital by default'* agenda (GOV.UK, 2016), the ripple of which is still yet to be fully felt across the range of p⬛⬛⬛⬛⬛⬛⬛⬛⬛⬛ the horizon there exists a very real risk of reactive approach⬛⬛⬛⬛⬛⬛⬛⬛⬛ould lead to digital exclusion, for both learners and educator⬛⬛⬛⬛⬛⬛⬛⬛nd methodologies are refashioned. It is important not to get so caught up with the need to reform that we lose sight of the impact of any reforms on the learner. Rust (2014, np) offers some early analysis on the dangers of technological reform in the populist context that can be easily transferred into the educational environment. She illuminates not only the magnitude of change ahead but also the consequences of getting it wrong. Furthermore, she provides a perspective on the disparity between those who 'have' and those who 'have not', those who 'can' and those who, for one reason or another, 'cannot', and it is here where education has a significant part to play.

Education and educators have historically been tasked with the role of equipping future generations with the knowledge and skills necessary to engage fully within society. It is for this reason that educators themselves must acquire knowledge relevant to developing technology-enhanced educational content, and more importantly the aptitude to deliver it in a manner that prepares students to participate in contemporary society. This is not to say that the old must be discarded in favour of the new, but to urge educators to proactively review practices to ensure that these are in line with learner needs in the connected age – bearing in mind, of course, as Heppell (2016) explains, that *'the thing about moving forward is deciding what to leave behind'* (p 6). Therefore, a measured approach to the digital shift is required. This in itself will go a long way towards reducing the potential for blanket educational approaches and generalised assumptions that often lead to the grouping of students into universal categories of description that can be far removed from their educational realities or future employment needs. For example, if we take the view that all learners are motivated, prepared and digitally equipped to learn in a uniform way, we are at risk of missing the mark. In this respect, we purposively avoid defaulting to the terms *'digital natives'* and *'digital immigrants'* (Prensky, 2001, p 3) in favour of the work of White and Le Cornu (2011), which takes a more fluid approach to thinking about digital engagement and capability.

Primary and, more so, post-compulsory education has made significant progress in terms of facilitating the development of digital literacies (Ofsted, 2011). However, as previously alluded to, providers across the breadth of the educational landscape have a long way to go before claims such as those made by Prensky ring true; particularly given the current disparate nature of digital exposure for learners across institutions. In addition, the array of digital capabilities across education, be that of those responsible for delivering it or for those expecting to receive it, signals in itself the need for change. The actuality of this was reflected in a recent UK government study that examined digital skills across the general populace, reporting a significant deficit in digital literacy across the nation on many levels (ECORYS UK, 2016). Therefore, it goes without saying that the time for reform is now (Heppell, 2016) and that sweeping approaches to curriculum design and delivery should be avoided, as this practice position negates the needs, and more importantly the complexity, of the 21st-century learner and the 21st-century learning landscape (Laurillard, cited in Beetham and Sharpe, 2007).

More often than not, curriculum construction that is technologically driven can be academically limiting and creatively stifling, particularly for cohorts with large student numbers (Pegrum et al, 2015). The second author's current research in the higher education context (Taylor, 2015) indicates that new does not always equate to improved and that broad stroke methods to embedding technologies within curriculum design can have an isolating, as opposed to the intended inclusive, effect, on a student's learning experience. Therefore, as educators, within the context of reform, we need to ensure that the design of blended learning spaces synchronises both, *'content and process ... [which are] compatible with [learners] ... and their social culture'* (Laurillard, cited in Beetham and Sharpe, 2007, p xvi). There are many examples of where this has been successfully achieved (McKean and Knight, 2016). You can read these in the linked report below.

The evolution of FELTAG: A glimpse of effective practice in UK further education and skills   http://repository.jisc.ac.uk/6325/1/The_evolution_of_FELTAG.pdf   (McKean and Knight, 2016).

As you will see, each of these practice examples evidence that when digital content and the use of technologies are matched with learner need the potential for disconnect can be avoided. McKean and Knight (2016) describe how *'meaningful and collaborative dialogue and partnership [with learners] ... can encourage a deeper understanding of how digital technology can support learners' needs'* (p 12). These types of participatory approaches encapsulate the essence of what the LearningWheel is: a model for crowdsourcing appropriate and practicable solutions to digital literacy, aimed at harnessing knowledge acquisition through engagement with emerging technologies (Torres and Guerrero,

2013). Given that, currently, technologies to a greater extent are driving change, the profile of the learner in terms of digital skill and ability must remain central to curriculum design, development and delivery. This is particularly relevant as we grapple with the speed and nature of said change – change that requires us to frequently revisit what it is that constitutes learning content and delivery in these digital times. Equally, if we are to strive towards a more digitally influenced philosophy, we need it to reconceptualise how we view ourselves as educators and to do this alongside the evolving educational landscape. It is our view that the digital explosion provides a perfect opportunity to do this and to do it well. We have found the LearningWheel, due to its collaborative and community orientation (Wenger, 2000), to have educational currency in this respect. It blends face-to-face teaching with online resources and spaces through the sourcing of tried-and-tested digital tools and content that can be adopted and adapted by *'networked teachers'* (Verhaart, 2012, p 191) for engaging with *'connected learners'* (Yang and Yuen, 2009, p 1).

CRITICAL **REFLECTION**

Thinking about reform and the learner, we ask you to reflect upon ...

- *the changes you have made or any you still need to make in terms of developing as a networked or global educator;*
- *and consider what it is that informs your thinking about the construction of teaching spaces for the learner in the connected age.*

Creatively engaging with the reform

Given that we have set the scene with regards to how we believe technological advancements are shaping education, and education's response to this, our focus moves to creativity and to how we believe this mindset to be central to future change (Robinson, 2006). Consequently, when we think about learning content we set it within the context of creativity, a position that aligns with the thinking of Brewer (2015), who explains how *'research has identified the importance and advantages of creative education'* and how this as an underpinning philosophy can increase *'student motivation, cooperation and self-confidence'* (p 3). Nonetheless, there are a number of barriers to creatively developing learning content and, more pointedly, learning content that includes the use of technologies, that we firstly wish to address. These are challenges that can, and seemingly do, impact upon a teacher's capacity to merge more traditional teaching and learning methods with those online. For Brewer (2015) these challenges are associated with policy-driven expectations, that when grouped with a lack of *'experience'*, and *'support'*, can lead to non-adoption and disengagement (p 4). Indeed, an Ofsted inspection of Virtual Learning Environments (VLEs) that found them to be inactive *'dumping grounds'* (2009, p 5) to some degree authenticates Brewer's thinking, in that findings such as these are often linked solely to teacher failure; a position that fails to recognise the wider system in which practice occurs. It is all too easy for a damaging narrative such as this to be introjected negatively by staff, and more significantly by management teams. It is a discourse which fails to acknowledge, for example, inadequate infrastructure or constraints on time; rhetoric that can be much more disabling to teachers than their lack of confidence or expertise in this emerging area of practice.

This is not to negate the fact that for some teachers, engagement with technology could be likened to navigating unchartered waters. There are copious accounts throughout the literature and particularly from within practice that evidences the difficulties with filling digital knowledge gaps, which in turn would reduce the digital divide. An acknowledgement of this is succinctly captured in the work of Koehler and Mishra (2009) who, when discussing 'Technological Pedagogical Content Knowledge' (TPCK) and educator professional development, explain that 'acquiring a new knowledge base and skill set can be challenging, particularly if it is a time-intensive activity that must fit into a busy schedule' (p 62). Interesting thus are the comments in the aforementioned Ofsted report that make reference to the conditions that support teacher development and good practice; these were environments where:

providers had provided their staff with a general introduction to the concept of VLEs, and then offered individuals encouragement in their curriculum area with more specialist detailed help when needed.

(Ofsted, 2009, p 6)

The above demonstrates the significance of ensuring that robust connections are made between teacher engagement, learning content, the learning environment and learning outcomes (Sharpe et al, 2006). Each influences the functioning of the other and in essence the overall effectiveness of the blended learning approach. Therefore, it is not surprising that we subscribe to the thinking of Garrison and Vaughan (2008, p 5), who urge educators to 'reject the dualistic thinking that seems to demand choosing between conventional face-to-face and online learning' in favour of a more 'integrated' approach. But equally, and in doing so, we challenge organisations who have overall responsibility for teaching delivery to provide the support that appears to be lacking for educators; support that would allow them to attend to their professional development in a way that speaks to the changing educational landscape and subsequent learner needs. The approach taken by Sharpe et al (2006) illustrates how, 'buy-in' can be achieved without defaulting to a dominant top–down 'strategy fatigue' type model of change (p 149). The LearningWheel model provides a context in which the barriers to creatively creating content for dissemination and delivery can be redressed. It can be used in a variety of ways to test, create, collate, map and share content for teaching and learning in the digital age. Like technology, it too is emerging, and as a model of digital pedagogy aims to facilitate and mirror the flexibility needed in the development of contemporary teaching practices. Later in this chapter, we provide visual examples of how content can be created by teachers for teachers, and in Chapter 2 we demonstrate technology-enhanced methods of delivery in further detail.

CRITICAL **REFLECTION**

Again we pause for thought and ask you to consider ...

- *the barriers to digital creativity in your teaching practice;*
- *your plans for embedding technologies into your teaching practice.*

Curating content: Reshaping the form

After touching on some of the drivers influencing educational reform and the barriers and possible solutions to creating technology-enhanced teaching spaces, we move on to discuss the way in which learning content to some degree has mutated as a result of technological advancements and make suggestions as to why these mutations are important. In addition, we reiterate the issue of digital literacy in relation to our abilities as educators to populate learning spaces with resources and materials appropriate to the needs of learners in the connected age. When we talk about learning content within the context of this book we refer to everything that teachers employ to generate knowledge acquisition. It is our view that, given the range of learning content now accessible and the amount of digital tools available, the construction of student-focused learning environments (those spaces where curriculum content generates learner curiosity and nurtures learner empowerment) is even more possible. These are dynamic spaces designed and created by visionary educators for whom the facilitation and co-production of knowledge are mediums through which student engagement and attainment can be achieved. As Ocker and Yaverbaum (1999) explain, *'many faculties have moved away from a teacher-centred lecture format for dispensing knowledge to a collaborative, student-centred environment for creating knowledge'* (p 427). This is quite the reverse of the previously held position, that more often than not saw the teacher as the dominant contributor of knowledge in the learning space. Some of our thinking here serves to further highlight points made earlier that explain the importance of understanding the learner in context and how significant this is to personalised learning, the development of intellectual curiosity, academic success or achievement more broadly in the connected age. We end this chapter by illustrating how the LearningWheel model is being used to create, curate and disseminate learning content, and provide an opportunity for readers to contribute to the development of a LearningWheel unique to this book.

Our discussion here is anticipatory and centred upon the notion of futuristic education – an era where educators are more likely to be thought of as *'networked teachers'* (Verhaart, 2012, p 191) and *'content curators'* (Susskind and Susskind, 2015, p 60), whose aim it is to develop and engage with *'connected learners'* (Yang and Yuen, 2009, p 1). While purposefully refraining from making definitive claims throughout this book about the 'best' ways forward, we do hold fast to the significance of human interaction within the learning context. In fact, the example offered earlier regarding virtual learning environments clearly highlights the implications of not having a systemic appreciation of all of the actors in a learning network (Mlitwa, 2007), and the role each plays in relation to the effectiveness of the learning space. This is a point we will revisit further in later chapters. For now it is suffice to say that educators, when thinking about the construction of learning spaces in the digital age, need to give significant thought to who and what is involved in an education network and that these considerations we suggest should also include digital literacy, digital confidence, materiality and the influence of each upon the other (Fenwick and Edwards, 2013). Thinking of this type is even more effective when aligned with the ongoing pursuit of professional development aimed at fulfilling the requirements of the contemporary classroom, because as Mihailidis and Cohen (2013, p 2) advise:

teachers at all levels of education must be prepared to negotiate the digital realities of their students as they design learning experiences around critical inquiry, analysis, and evaluation. Indeed, educators today have a certain responsibility to focus student skills and experiences in an exercise of participation with the surrounding media.

Therefore, an appreciation of the digital realities of learners must begin with an appraisal of the individual teacher and institutional digital capacities, or the risk of othering occurs. The reflective mapping exercise provided in the introduction provides a useful starting point. It is our belief that it is only when we as educators have confronted our own digital truths that we can move to consider those of our learners. From these understandings we can develop the insights necessary for effective learner engagement in a digital sense, and central to this are the skills to collate, curate and navigate learning content in a computer-mediated age.

The term *content curation* has been more commonly associated with the work of museum curators and librarians due to the way in which they go about the business of logging, managing and monitoring collections, be those artefacts or books. The internet age, as with lots of other things, has adopted and adapted the term mainly because of the volume of content made available through the web and the aptitude required for the filtering of relevant and valid content (Weiler, 2005). As noted, curating relevant and effective learning content is not new; you do not need us to explain in any great detail about how this skill has historically been central to the educator role. However, what has and is changing is the learning context, the learner and more broadly the form of curriculum content that will meet the needs of the 21st-century learner. In this respect it is not helpful to think in fixed terms, or as we mentioned earlier, to dismiss the old in place of the new. In fact, the most relevant learning content in the connected age is that which merges what was found to be effective in the old with what we are finding to be effective in terms of the new; while carefully evaluating the impact of both on the learning experience and learning outcomes on an ongoing basis. This unsurprisingly, and rightly so, still involves theories such as *'constructive alignment'* (Biggs, 1996, p 347). Previous to the influx of technologies as a means to collating and sharing resources, educators might have selected or produced learning content which they alone judged to be relevant to the subject matter and presented this to learners in hard copy form within a physical space. They would filter that which 'they' believed pertinent to knowledge acquisition in terms of the overarching learning outcomes and then offered this content to learners for perusal prior to, during or post the learning event. However, given the access to information that the world wide web affords, it is much more difficult to assess what learners 'themselves' bring to the learning space and to establish what it is that they truly require from it.

Therefore, there exists a very real opportunity to redress the risk of the construction of learning spaces that are learner limiting, particularly when learners have the access they do to subject-relevant material, which in essence means that they could arrive at the learning context knowing more or, if not, as much, as the educator does. Contrary to this are the conversations that still persist along academic corridors that cite students as passive or ambivalent in relation to knowledge acquisition (Weiler, 2005). We believe these generalisations to be dangerous and dismissive because to pontificate in this respect denies the actuality of *'informal learning'* and how it is this form of learning that can be used to stimulate curiosity (Mason and Rennie, 2007, p 197). Access to informal learning in the digital era takes many forms, be that a blog post, tweet, video, vlog, story, the opinions of Facebook connections or information gleaned through some other form of virtual social space. The skill it takes to reduce a doctorate to a three-minute presentation, aptly titled 'The Three Minute Thesis' that can be seen via the link below emphasises how information, in such digestible forms, not only encourages engagement with learning content but also makes it extremely accessible in the age of information overload.

The Three Minute Thesis http://threeminutethesis.org/ (The University of Queensland, 2008).

Even that which could be perceived as minimal interaction with the information highway can result in the construction of knowledge. It could, of course, be argued that information has always been readily available to students prior to the digital age and this is true. However, the reach, range and access to information that the internet provides means that we might have to pay attention to learning content in a more judicious manner. Not only does the internet provide access to a wide range of learning content, it also allows educators to co-create learning resources with learners; and this does not always need to happen within a classroom. It might be that the whole notion of the classroom needs to be revised, in terms of what it is, where it is and how we are to work with it as our digital knowledge progresses. It is worthwhile taking the time to explore platforms such as Wordpress, GoogleDrive, GoogleDocs, Storify, there are many more, to consider how you might utilise these digital tools and resources to create content and to nurture the co-production of knowledge with learners.

The content shared on the LearningWheel website is a useful starting point for exploring digital resources (Figure 1.1) and as noted it serves to provide opportunities to trial and test technologies for practice. We subscribe to a *'collate, curate, communicate to create and collaborate'* way of thinking about learning content. We see educators employing digital methods from across the four modes of engagement, through the three modes of delivery (Figure i), to enable them to effectively collate and curate content, which is then communicated to create knowledge in collaboration with colleagues and students. This is a position akin to the work of Nerantzi and Beckingham (2015), whose *'5Cs'* methodology provides an experiential context in which to develop as a digitally orientated educator (p 112). As you will see, the LearningWheel offers an additional space in which to engage in this type of method due to its multidimensional and blended nature.

There is, of course, another side to the volume of information made available through the internet, which can have the opposite effect on engagement, and it is here where content curation becomes even more important (Verhaart, 2012). Take, for example, situations where, with the best of intentions, learners are provided with a number of web links designed to support learning in relation to a particular topic; there is a significant chance, due to the incredible amount of material available, that they could feel overwhelmed. This is comparable in old money to the circulation of unwieldy reading lists with an assumption made that learners will know how to prioritise said reading. In contrast, in the new world, a considerably more helpful method of distributing learning content is first to collate it, curate it and then break it down into manageable chunks under headings such as those that might be seen in the reading list section of a module handbook: 'recommended reading, supplementary reading, core reading' or something similar.

Part of the academic journey is the acquisition of skills that eventually lead learners to be independent of the educator in terms of screening and selecting material relevant to their studies, but more often than not these skills take some time to develop. Some of the digital resources, as pointed out earlier, that are freely available can be embedded within learning activities to enable learners to become the curators of their own content. A few more examples of digital resources that can be used as content repositories are YouTube, Padlet and iBooks, all of which are incredibly useful to both educators and students as knowledge hubs (Figure 1.1). It is through appropriate content curation that educators can model the skills students need to collate subject-specific content. In this respect, where there exists a large amount of subject-relevant material educators must curate and be directional in their communication so as not to confuse or to add to what can often appear like a daunting task.

CRITICAL **REFLECTION**

Thinking about learning content and blended learning, we ask you to reflect upon ...

- *the ways you have historically curated learning content;*
- *how (or if) your approach has changed;*
- *which blended learning approaches you use.*

Given that we aim to make this book as interactive as practicable so that it is as experiential as possible, without further delay we move to introduce the 'Learning Content' mode of the LearningWheel (Figure 1.1) with an attached web link that will take you to an example of a wheel in its totality. The learning content in this mode of engagement is made up from the digital resources that teachers have used to support and generate learning. It is important to be aware that as technology advances the types and scope of digital resources and access to learning content will also advance. This is why we come to this book with an open mind and hope that you will too, as the characteristics and form of education is most likely to keep changing in ways that we have never quite experienced before. Educators must, therefore, be critical in their choice and use of digital resources, to ensure that those selected are fit for purpose. This again is where the LearningWheel is unique as it consists of content that has been previously employed for teaching and learning by colleagues, who are clear about its purpose within their area of practice.

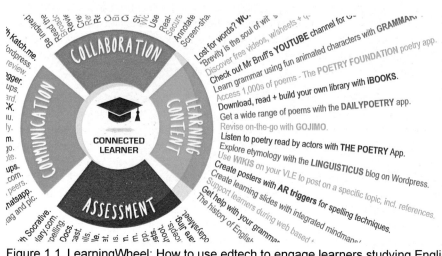

Figure 1.1 LearningWheel: How to use edtech to engage learners studying English.

How to use edtech to engage learners studying English http://learningwheel.co.uk/ 2016/06/english-language/ (Kellsey, 2015).

The above graphic, 'How to use edtech to engage learners studying English' (Figure 1.1), is one of a growing collection of subject-specific LearningWheels that have been developed collaboratively by a community of English teachers. Pedagogically the LearningWheel, more broadly, is informed by notions of curation, collaboration, engagement, mentoring and peer support. The idea is that the most informed source of support for teachers, whether new to the profession or new to technologies, is from that of a knowledgeable peer – a colleague who is more likely to understand the nuances of a specific field of practice and the demands of the target audience. We will come back to the topic of collaboration in Chapter 3.

However, here, as you can see in Figure 1.1, contributors to the 'Learning Content' section of this LearningWheel have suggested a range of digital tools and resources that have been used to engage learners with subject-specific knowledge. The learning potential here, however, is twofold in nature and often unrecognised. For example, the spoke that suggests using 'The Poetry App' signposts to learning content relevant to students studying English; however, at the same time it presents the opportunity to upload the app, navigate the app and to become familiar with a digital process. In contrast, a spoke that suggests a game-based application geared towards the *'enhancement of motivation and engagement in learning tasks'* (Caponetto et al, 2014, p 55) has quite a different focus in terms of the learning process.

Accordingly, choosing digital resources requires significant criticality, to ensure that the shiny and new ideologies do not override purposeful usage in the learning context. The resources suggested by teachers, and at times educational technologists, across each of the LearningWheels are generally evidence based and varied in nature and are shared using the web platform GoogleDocs. One of the most unique features of this collaborative process is the way that subject and technology-specific knowledge are simultaneously made available. Thus, the use of digital tools to access learning content provides the opportunity for educators and learners to become familiar with digital methods that subsequently facilitate the development of digital capabilities. This duality widens access to the range of knowledge at one's disposal.

It is our plan to construct a LearningWheel through our readership that identifies the most useful digital resources and apps used to date across education. The link below will take you directly to a GoogleDoc on the LearningWheel website that is unique to this book.

LearningWheel Book: Top Apps and Resources

https://docs.google.com/spreadsheets/d/1EDRN4UaR6m93B_YEMGTZ8EOISI WnfWsENkcDByWtWIM/edit#gid=2134954465 (Kellsey and Taylor, 2016, np).

We would encourage you to visit this link so that you too can contribute to this teaching and learning resource. If you do decide to make a contribution, you will be cited on the website as a contributor to this LearningWheel and like all of those who have previously been involved, will be acknowledged as having shaped a little more of our digital development as a global teaching collective, otherwise known as a *'community of practice'* (Mina, 2006, p 143).

As you might have already noticed if you have clicked on the link above, there are four modes of engagement, each of which are open and awaiting your suggestions. There will be an opportunity to populate each of the other modes of engagement as we weave through each chapter. For now, we are focussing on the learning content element of the model and offer the visual guide in Figure 1.2 to assist you to populate the GoogleDoc. In short, what you need to do is to decide which digital tool or resource you wish to share within the 'Learning Content' mode of engagement and describe in a short sentence *what* resource you use, *how* you use it and *why* you use it. The LearningWheel posted above and those on the website illustrate colleagues' contributions; the content of these completed spokes will assist you to make your contribution. Once you have formulated your suggestion all you need to do is click on one of the available spaces on the spreadsheet and post your contribution, along with your name, or identifier if you are using your Twitter handle. There is also space for you to add details of your employing institution if you so wish.

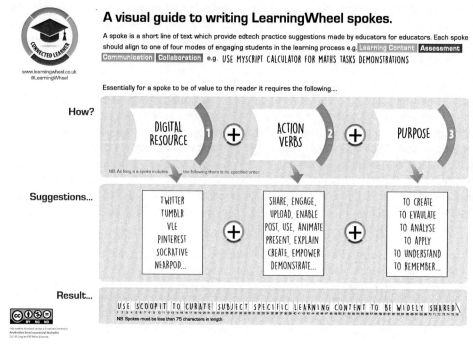

Figure 1.2 LearningWheel: A visual guide to writing LearningWheel spokes.

A visual guide to writing LearningWheel spokes http://learningwheel.co.uk/about-learningwheel/writing-learningwheel-spoke/ (Kellsey, 2016).

If you have made a contribution, you will have experienced the LearningWheel in its fullness and it is now that you can claim your membership of this globally situated Virtual Community of Learning and Practice (VCoL&P) (Allen et al, 2003). Welcome!

CRITICAL **REFLECTION**

Thinking specifically about Learning Content and blended learning, we ask you reflect upon ...

- *the digital tools and content you are using or might wish to use in the creation of 'blended learning' spaces.*

So what we have discussed is how the system, including the educator, the environment, the learner, and the form of learning content and access to it, have changed. We have reflected upon possible barriers and blocks to creativity, described what learning content is in the connected age and have shown how the LearningWheel can provide a space for thinking creatively about said content. Further change, however, is inevitable, and as with anything practices and trends evolve, mutate and sometimes drop away completely. Without going into a philosophical discussion about the nature of change, in essence, the only certainty is that almost everything in our world takes on a new form or at least shifts in terms of meaning. Technology is doing a wonderful job at metaphorically keeping us all on our toes! And incidentally on the subject of toes, as random as this may seem, given the progress in the field of robotics we could argue that even the mere toe has taken on a new form and new meaning as we hear of robots walking across restaurants, as was reported recently in Business UK by Peterson (2016, np), to take food orders. Around the same time, indeed, just two days before this article came to light, the large fast food institution that is McDonalds issued a piece in the same publication (Taylor, 2016, np) that indicated an increase in automation over humans in the delivery of their services. We will leave you with these thoughts, as this perhaps is a conversation for another time. It is, however, enough to say that both these articles evidence the speed and direction in which the world is evolving and this is a world where nothing can be left to chance. Therefore, as educators, we need to hold firm to our commitment to the development of critical, analytical and connected thinkers for whom questioning and curiosity is the default no matter what the medium. We need to do this while ensuring that we ourselves are equipped with the necessary skills to impart and co-construct knowledge. In relation to this mode of engagement, these are the abilities to curate learning content that allows for the aforementioned type of learner development to occur.

REFERENCES

Allen, S, Ure, D and Evans, S (2003) *Virtual Communities of Practice as Learning Networks*. Masie Center, e-Learning Consortium, Brigham Young University, Instructional Psychology and Technology.

Biggs, J (1996) Enhancing Teaching through Constructive Alignment. *Higher Education*, 32(3): 347–64.

Brewer, G (2015) Introduction: Creativity and Education, in Brewer, G and Hogarth, R (eds) *Creative Education, Teaching and Learning: Creativity, Engagement and the Student Experience*, pp 1–8. London: Palgrave Macmillan.

Buckingham, D (2007) *Beyond Technology: Children's Learning in the Age of Digital Culture*. Cambridge and Malden: Polity Press.

Caponetto, I, Earp, J and Ott, M (2014) Gamification and Education: A Literature Review, in *ECGBL 2014: Eighth European Conference on Games Based Learning*. [online] Available at: www.itd.cnr.it/download/gamificationECGBL2014.pdf (accessed 14 August 2016).

Department for Business Innovation and Skills (BIS) (2014) *Government Response to the Recommendations from the Further Education Learning Technology Action Group (FELTAG)*. 1st ed. [e-book]. [online]. Available at: www.gov.uk/government/uploads/system/uploads/attachment_data/file/320242/bis-14-841-government-response-to-recommendations-from-the-FELTAG-action-plan.pdf (accessed 6 May 2015).

Department for Business Innovation and Skills (BIS) (2015) FELTAG Progress Report: An Update on Progress since the Publication of the Further Education Learning Technologies Action Group (FELTAG). [online] Available at: www.gov.uk/government/uploads/system/uploads/attachment_data/file/405001/BIS_15_71_FELTAG_progress_report.pdf (accessed 1 April 2016).

ECORYS UK (2016) Digital Skills for the UK Economy. [online] Available at: www.gov.uk/government/uploads/system/uploads/attachment_data/file/492889/DCMSDigitalSkillsReportJan2016.pdf (accessed 30 June 2016).

Fenwick, T and Edwards, R (2013) Performative Ontologies: Sociomaterial Approaches to Researching Adult Education and Lifelong Learning. *European Journal for Research on the Education and Learning of Adults*, 4(1): 49–63.

Garrison, D R and Vaughan, N D (2008) *Blended Learning in Higher Education: Framework, Principles and Guidelines*. San Francisco, CA: Jossey-Bass.

GOV.UK (2016) Digital by Default Service Standard. [online] Available at: www.gov.uk/service-manual/digital-by-default (accessed 30 May 2016).

Heppell, S (2016) Education Technology Action Group (ETAG): Our Reflections. [online] Available at: www.heppell.net/etag/media/ETAG_reflections.pdf (accessed 30 June 2016).

Kellsey, D (2015) LearningWheel: How to use a range of digital resources to engage learners studying English. [online] Available at: http://learningwheel.co.uk/2016/06/english-language/ (accessed 1 June 2016).

Kellsey, D (2016) LearningWheel: A visual guide to writing LearningWheel spokes. [online] Available at: http://learningwheel.co.uk/about-learningwheel/writing-learningwheel-spoke/ (accessed 15 August 2016).

Kellsey, D and Taylor, A M L (2016) LearningWheel Book: Top Apps and Resources. [online] Available at: https://docs.google.com/spreadsheets/d/1EDRN4UaR6m93B_YEMGTZ8EOISIWnfWsENkcDByWtWlM/edit#gid=2134954465 (accessed 30 August 2016).

Koehler, M and Mishra, P (2009) What is Technological Pedagogical Content Knowledge (TPACK)? *Contemporary Issues in Technology and Teacher Education*, 9(1): 60–70.

Lambert, N (2014) FELTAG Recommendations: Paths Forward to a Digital Future for Further Education and Skills. [online] Available at: http://feltag.org.uk/wp-content/uploads/2012/01/FELTAG-REPORT-FINAL.pdf (accessed 2 April 2016).

Laurillard, D (2007) Preface, in Beetham, H and Sharpe, R (2013) (eds) *Rethinking Pedagogy for a Digital Age: Designing and Delivering E-Learning*, pp xix–xxi. London: Routledge.

Mason, R and Rennie, F (2007) Using Web 2.0 for Learning in the Community. *The Internet and Higher Education*, 10(3): 196–203.

McKean, P and Knight, S (2016) The Evolution of FELTAG: A Glimpse at Effective Practice in UK Further Education and Skills. [online] Available at: http://repository.jisc.ac.uk/6325/1/The_evolution_of_FELTAG.pdf (accessed 1 April 2016).

McLoughlin, C and Lee, M J W (2010) Personalised and Self Regulated Learning in the Web 2.0 Era: International Exemplars of Innovative Pedagogy Using Social Software. *Australasian Journal of Educational Technology*, 26(1): 28–43.

Mihailidis, P and Cohen, J (2013) Exploring Curation as a Core Competency in Digital and Media Literacy Education. *Journal of Interactive Media in Education*, 1(2): 1–19.

Mina, C. (2006) Communities of Practice: An Alternative Learning Model for Knowledge Creation. *British Journal of Educational Technology*, 37(1): 143–46.

Mlitwa, N (2007) Technology for Teaching and Learning in Higher Education Contexts: Activity Theory and Actor Network Theory Analytical Perspectives Using ICT. *International Journal of Education and Development*, 3(4). [online] Available at: http://ijedict.dec.uwi.edu/viewarticle.php?id=420%layout=html (accessed 3 September 2016).

Nerantzi, C and Beckingham, S (2015) BYOD4L: Learning to Use Own Smart Devices for Learning and Teaching through the 5C Framework, in Middleton, A (ed) *Smart Learning: Teaching and Learning with*

Smartphones and Tablets in Post-compulsory Education. Sheffield: MELSIG publication. [online] Available at: http://shura.shu.ac.uk/9616/ (accessed 19 September 2016).

Ocker, R J and Yaverbaum, G J (1999) Asynchronous Computer-Mediated Communication versus Face-to-Face Collaboration: Results on Student Learning, Quality and Satisfaction. *Group Decision and Negotiation*, 8(5): 427–40.

Ofsted (2009) Virtual Learning Environments: An Evaluation of their Development in a Sample of Educational Settings. [online] Available at: http://dera.ioe.ac.uk/325/1/VLE%20an%20evaluation%20of%20their%20development.pdf (accessed 2 June 2016).

Ofsted (2011) ICT in schools 2008–11: An Evaluation of Information and Communication Technology Education in Schools in England 2008–11. [online] Available at: www.gov.uk/government/uploads/system/uploads/attachment_data/file/181223/110134.pdf (accessed 14 June 2016).

Pegrum, M, Bartle, E and Longnecker, N (2015) Can Creative Podcasting Promote Deep Learning? The Use of Podcasting for Learning Content in an Undergraduate Science Unit. *British Journal of Educational Technology*, 46 (1): 142–52.

Peterson, H (2016) Pizza Hut just signaled a terrifying reality for fast-food workers. [online] Available at: http://uk.businessinsider.com/pizza-hut-employs-pepper-robot-workers-2016-5?r=US&IR=T (accessed 6 June 2016).

Prensky, M (2001) Digital Natives, Digital Immigrants: Part 1. *On the Horizon*, 9(5): 1–6.

Robinson, K (2006) Ken Robinson: Do schools kill creativity? [online] Available at: www.ted.com/talks/ken_robinson_says_schools_kill_creativity (accessed 3 September 2016).

Rust, E (2014) When the UK goes 'digital by default', who will be left behind? *The Guardian*. [online] Available at: www.theguardian.com/technology/2014/jun/23/when-the-uk-goes-digital-by-default-who-will-be-left-behind (accessed 10 June 2016).

Sharpe, R, Benfield, G and Francis, R (2006) Implementing a University E-Learning Strategy: Levers for Change within Academic Schools. *Research in Learning Technology*, 14(2): 135–51.

Susskind, R E and Susskind, D (2015) *The Future of the Professions: How Technology Will Transform the Work of Human Experts*. Oxford: Open University Press.

Taylor, A M L (2015) Exploring the contribution of social work education to the digital socialisation of students for practice. [online] Available at: https://drive.google.com/open?id=0B8EjX-OzeLTaMGtiVWFIVU1qYzQ (accessed 10 April 2016).

Taylor, K (2016) McDonald's ex-CEO just revealed a terrifying reality for fast-food workers. [online] Available at: http://uk.businessinsider.com/mcdonalds-ex-ceo-takes-on-minimum-wage-2016-5?r=US&IR=T (accessed 6 June 2016).

The University of Queensland (2008) Three Minute Thesis (3MT®). [online] Available at: http://threeminutethesis.org/index.html (accessed 20 June 2016).

Torres, A and Guerrero, C (2013) Learning Content Development with Social Tools: Learning Generated Content in Engineering. *IEEE-RITA Latin American Learning Technologies Journal*, 8(3): 111–18.

Verhaart, M (2012) Curating Digital Content in Teaching and Learning Using Wiki Technology. *Proceedings of the 12th IEEE International Conference on Advanced Learning Technologies, ICALT*, pp 191–93.

Weiler, A (2005) Information-Seeking Behavior in Generation Y Students: Motivation, Critical Thinking, and Learning Theory. *The Journal of Academic Librarianship*, 31(1): 46–53.

Wenger, E (2000) *Communities of Practice: Learning, Meaning, and Identity*. Cambridge: Cambridge University Press.

White, D S and Le Cornu, A (2011) Visitors and Residents: A new typology for online engagement. [online] Available at: http://firstmonday.org/ojs/index.php/fm/article/view/3171/3049 (accessed 10 June 2016).

Yang, H H and Yuen, S C (eds) (2009) *Collective Intelligence and E-Learning 2.0: Implications of Web-Based Communities and Networking*. Hershey, PA: IGI Global.

Mode, medium, message…

In this chapter, we consider the ways in which communication styles and methods within the education context have and are evolving as a result of the connected age. We offer possible solutions to some of these changes through drawing on examples of technology-enhanced learning from the LearningWheel Virtual Community of Learning and Practice (VCoL&P) to illustrate how the use of technologies to communicate and engage can increase the learning potential within a teaching space. Additionally, these practice accounts evidence the way in which the use of technologies can bridge digital knowledge gaps, for both teachers and learners (Instefjord and Munthe, 2016). We again avoid 'either or' type scenarios in favour of blended approaches (Garrison and Vaughan, 2008) and reflect upon what has gone before so that we can better understand more about where we are now. In doing so, many of the methods we present marry former teaching and learning practices with those that are emerging.

As technology-engaged educators we are acutely aware of the debates and discussions being communicated across the sector relating to modern technologies and their relationship to education. Concerns are multilayered, but more generally they question the appropriateness of the use of technologies in everyday teaching practices. The work of @BryanMMathers (https://twitter.com/BryanMMathers) is incredibly helpful here, with his *'Visual Thinkery'* providing graphic representations of the current technology-infused learning landscape, images that are peppered with insights into some of the wider conversations being had and practice methods being adopted (Mathers, 2016). We continue to choose the path of least resistance in our respective roles, working 'with' as opposed to against the tide of technological change; accepting it as ongoing, at times relentless, but above all 'necessary'. Inasmuch as we appreciate the difficulties that social media type technologies can pose in the educational context, our rationale for embracing them is very much based upon an understanding of the centrality of communication in education, its significance to life-stage development, and the benefits of having a range of mediums through which this essential individuation can be achieved.

Communication, outside of the educational setting, remains central to how we access and make sense of the world, and modern technologies are now more than ever intrinsic to this. It takes many forms and is fundamental to human socialisation. It begins the day we are born and involves intra- and interpersonal exchanges that are formative in terms of how we learn to navigate, construct and value knowledge. Interactions occur at macro, micro and meso levels (Bronfenbrenner, 2009) throughout the life course, shaping our cognitions, communicative abilities and relationships thereafter. They are core to who we become and how we negotiate life. Thus, the messages we receive and mediums through which we receive them have a bearing on not only our individuation but also on our ability to function as participatory citizens. As Simon (1999, cited in Hargie and Dickson, 2004, p 8) explains:

people's own identity and meaningful existence depend on finding a place in the social world. The ability to achieve this 'place', in turn, depends to a very large extent on one's interactive skills.

Formal education is incredibly important to this interconnected journey of self-actualisation (Rogers, 1957). It is the medium through which much of our ability to communicate is influenced and formed. It plays a central role in our maturation as social beings and is significant to how we subsequently experience and are experienced in the world. As noted, in the introductory chapter, educational processes require ongoing evaluation to ensure that they continue to offer learning experiences that are fit for purpose. With regards to communication, these learning experiences routinely include exposure to a range of interpersonal exchanges that are designed to equip learners with knowledge, and the skills necessary for engagement with the wider world. The world we refer to is, however, more technologically orientated and digitally reliant than ever before, and it is, therefore, essential that we grasp opportunities to develop technical skills within the learning context. What we are suggesting here we have already highlighted in Chapter 1 (p 13), where we talked about exploiting the potential within a learning activity to attend not only to subject-specific learning but to do this in a way that also develops digital literacies. This, of course, requires the *'presence'* (Rettie, 2004) of technologies within curriculum content, in a manner that would see them threaded where appropriate throughout lesson design and delivery. Inasmuch as we accept that as a profession we are not quite there yet or fully comfortable with digitisation, we hope to convince colleagues that the absence of modern technologies is no longer an option, that is, if we are to educate and prepare learners for the realities of the future.

Reflecting on the different ways that access to the modern world has changed leaves us in little doubt that the fabric of the social world will continue to transform. There are copious examples of these transformations, some more subtle than others, that have had quite a bearing on how we exist. We again return your attention to the predictions of the Susskinds (2015) cited earlier in the book, whose findings pose a challenge to educators in terms of the direction of future travel. They ask important and valid questions about what we assume it is that we are educating 21st-century learners to become. Implicit in their musings is the need for change. Helpful to any forecasting for the future, however, is a mulling over of the past, and in relation to current communication methods this includes thinking through the ways in which automated systems are progressing, and how this progression is significantly replacing human intervention and interaction. Take some of the more essential public utilities: gas, water, electricity and how access to these amenities are now only possible through an online exchange. Stark also is the number of self-service machines situated in places where once upon a time a human teller would have sat. Reassuring, for now, is the fact that when one of these machines fails or malfunctions an 'actual' human being comes to its rescue. Nonetheless, the loss of human interaction to a remote online transaction or self-service is only set to increase, and we would defy anyone to deny that they have not experienced at least one online interaction that has caused them to purport the superiority of man over the machine (Benedictus, 2016). Even though this might be the case, the point here is that engagement no longer relies solely on human input (Hanson, 2016). Communication is no longer bounded or boundaried (Young and Muller, 2010). Increasingly it occurs via a mobile device (Przybylski and Weinstein, 2013); classrooms are no longer local (Patterson et al, 2011); geography as a term is being replaced in favour of 'connectography' (Khanna, 2016); and employability now requires a distinct set of digital skills (Blackwood, 2016).

All of this evidences the extent to which technologies are influencing the lived experience and as a consequence are shaping the skills required to access and engage with the world that is, in essence, becoming a much more remote and virtual place. Indisputable therefore is the fact that the current digital shift is proving to be one of the most demanding drivers experienced by educators and the education system since its inception. Long gone are the days where face-to-face or real-time communications dominated and undeniable is the fact that an increasing amount of communication occurs online or in a virtual sense (Warschauer, 2001). Yet, not everyone views computer-mediated communication (CMC) or the idea of digital connectedness positively. A significant number of educators remain unconvinced and suspicious about technologies (Hennessy et al, 2005), and to some degree rightly so ... that is, if this hesitancy relates to the risks of putting the technology before the pedagogy (Watson, 2001).

The volume and at times the complexity of digital resources materialising are in equal measures shaping how learners communicate, engage with and acquire knowledge. This, therefore, poses even more challenges for teachers, teaching, and of course for the learners themselves; and in itself should be reason enough to prompt an appraisal of the methods being used in education to engage students and communicate learning content. Again, what is integral to this is a thorough understanding of how communication skills are acquired, where communication occurs and the thinking through of how unhelpful it might actually be to require learners to disengage from what is increasingly becoming one of their primary mediums for communicating. Expecting learners to adhere to a 'digital switch-off' (Cotter, 2015) once they arrive through the school gates could mean that we lose out on an opportunity to develop digital literacy relevant to education and to future employment. This is not to say that CMC should be the primary means of communicating but to urge colleagues to continue to examine how the digital behaviours of learners can be exploited in terms of maximising the possibilities for teaching communication skills in the educational environment. Communication methods used to engage across the range of educational contexts will be varied. Nonetheless, what is important is that current practices are being scrutinised to ensure that they are purposive in terms of the interpersonal exchanges deemed to be effective for knowledge acquisition in education. Learning experiences will prepare learners to communicate effectively, and to a degree safely, in the modern world. As long as we remain true to the idea that 'dazzling and new does not always equate to improved', we can feel reassured that we are being critical in our choices and eventual approaches.

CRITICAL **REFLECTION**

Reflecting on a communication methods list ...

- *Think about your preferred methods and how these might have changed over the years.*
- *Note the ways in which technologies have shaped how you communicate both personally and professionally.*
- *Can you remember the first communication technology you ever used? Do you still use it?*

From caves to classrooms and beyond

Prior to the current expeditious nature of technological advancement, human interaction outside of the verbal exchange took many forms. Methods of communication were developed and utilised in a manner that reflected the culture, the economy and educational agendas of the time. We have innovations such as hieroglyphics, the Phoenician alphabet, the Gutenberg printing press and the telephone, to name a few, to thank for how far we have come. Early communication innovations were initially sporadic, with new methods emerging in response to what were thought to be the needs and demands of the populace. In some ways, they set the tone for what was to come. Post, what were groundbreaking inventions of their time, the pace and functionality of technologies and their usage took a substantial leap. The internet emerged, with all its offshoots proclaiming to offer even more exciting and efficient ways of connecting, sharing and communicating information. With each new invention came much excitement but more often than not much resistance, the latter on most occasions taking precedence. A comment elicited from the residents of a London suburbia captured by Stein (1996) in a study that considered responses to the introduction of the telephone aptly captures the historic and to a degree the ongoing resistance to technological change. The participants in this study believed that it was, *'useless to fight against the inevitable'* exclaiming that a *'day ... [would] come when we shall all be on the telephone'* (Stein, 1996, p 10). What is interesting here is that this type of reaction to technological advancement is not unique to the 1900s; it has been a feature across most, if not all of the generations. The introduction of train travel in the 1800s, for example, led to fears about the future of the coach and the canal industry. Alongside these worries were concerns about safety, relating to the fact that this newly found form of commuting would exceed speeds of 30 mph. The issue of speed was not only thought of as incredibly dangerous but also deeply unnecessary. More recently we seem to be preoccupied with the introduction of robotics (Alimisis and Kynigos, 2009), artificial intelligence (Wenger, 2014) and the increased use of text speech (Dansieh, 2011). The decline of handwriting is another area of debate, with the perceived lost art of conversation (Turkle, 2015) being talked about as one of the most damaging blows of the digital age. There are many more examples; however, our aim here is simply to provide a flavour of the concerns and the nature of resistance that can co-exist when new technologies are introduced and embedded into our everyday existence. Unsurprisingly due to the magnitude of change occurring, the internet, social media and technologies more broadly continue to cause concern, generate criticism and evoke unease; and the resultant anxieties are not solely located within the popularist context. There are examples too from within education.

A significant percentage of educators express reservations in relation to the purpose and use of technolog   d in some cases beyond, the classroom. There are those   ial media usage in class time distracts, detracts and dilu   acquisition in the learning space. There is research to support these beliefs (Ravizza et al, 2014). However, polar to this argument are studies that show how mobile devices can support and complement traditional classroom methods (Attewell, 2005). Learner attention has always been an issue for educators (Rogers, 2015), and inasmuch as technologies can be distracting, they are not fully to blame. Reflecting back on our own educational experiences, we each remember times when we would 'doodle' while in lessons due to a loss of concentration or through being distracted for one reason or another. It is not unusual for learners to communicate using what are often thought of as disruptive behaviours. Non-engagement and other signs of disengagement, however, dare we say it, are more likely to be borne out of boredom or frustration rather than related solely to a digital device itself (Stephens and Pantoja, 2016).

This is not to dismiss the fact that as a population we are becoming increasingly attached, or as some have found, addicted to our digital devices (Turkle, 2015; Ofcom, 2016). We each find it deeply uncomfortable and quite unnecessary that our own children often feel the need to impose technology bans on 'us' and can we just say that we are more than happy that you ascribe an appropriate emoticon in response to this revelation; hopefully, of course, in our favour! Moving swiftly on, the fact is that we all have still some way to go before digital technologies are not viewed with suspicion when present in learning spaces, that the digital shift is fully embraced and that we view digital scholarship (Costa, 2014) as part of what we 'do'. While it is difficult, and to a larger extent unnecessary, to prescribe practice methods at this stage of our understanding, it is suffice to say that securing a balanced perspective will be key to how we develop methodologies that reflect contemporary teaching for learners and learning in the connected age.

Another phase of the digital shift is well and truly upon us and communication strategies and the mediums for imparting information are the focus here. Communication has always been key to curriculum delivery and engagement. Understanding how learning content needs to be communicated and who it is being communicated to should be central to how we rethink curriculum design, development and delivery in the digital age. We have already provided an overview in Chapter 1 about the importance of reconceptualising the construct of the 21st-century learner and learning environment and here we relate this to how the curriculum is communicated, where it is communicated and outline resources that can support communication with learners of the digital age. No longer can it be assumed that face-to-face or didactic (Blin and Munro, 2008) methods of imparting knowledge and information are the only appropriate means to engagement nor should they continue to dominate the learning experience or learning spaces. Hard copy and forms of physical resources are now seen to be a thing of the past, but then again there have been recent reports of learners discussing email in old and outdated terms (Kolowich, 2011). Even though digital capabilities are still not formally assessed, learners are being exposed to a range of digital communication type technologies within informal settings and through informal means. More often than not, they are connecting in one way or another through a social media platform on various forms of digital devices and even though exposure is of an informal nature, this type of communication is thought to be quite formative for an increasing amount of the student population (Bullard, 2011).

There are a number of platforms in use that are currently available to learners. You may be aware of most of them: Facebook, Snapchat, LinkedIn, Instagram, Twitter, YouTube, Google+, Pinterest, Tumblr, WhatsApp ... the list goes on. Whether or not as educators, we find these social spaces appropriate or educational they are nonetheless increasingly replacing the more physical type locations where communication once may have occurred. They are a significant part of social life and are spaces where communication skills in one form or another are being shaped. As educators we will have formed opinions about the usefulness, safeness or validity of these spaces. However, until formal and compulsory education systems consistently embed the development of digital literacies into the curriculum and Initial Teacher Training we are always going to be filling the gaps. Usage and knowledge about technology usage will remain disparate, and subsequently students will not be able to evidence the digital capabilities required by future employers (Myers et al, 2014). Therefore, we should make full use of Beckingham's (2015, p 1) point that draws our attention to the fact that through exposure to everyday technologies we are 'engaging in informal learning without realising it', because it is making the implicit explicit that will enable us as educators to take advantage of and utilise digital influences on the learning landscape to drive student gain.

CRITICAL **REFLECTION**

Reflecting on your teacher training and professional development list ...

- *Think about the technologies you were introduced to for communication purposes and those that you have used throughout your professional life.*
- *Which has been most useful or most effective in terms of your role and learning outcomes?*
- *Are there any others that you are considering using?*

Communication: The *what*, the *how* and the *why*?

In Chapter 1 we provided detail about how contributions to a LearningWheel are made. In this section of the book we add further depth due to the fact that the act of contributing to a LearningWheel is a form of communication and fits perfectly with illustrating this mode of engagement. But firstly we feel it necessary to briefly return to the centrality of communication within education because it is our belief that in the absence of effective communication, learning is simply not possible. It is essential to engagement and key to how connections are made. It creates a sense of belonging and facilitates the building of relationships with educators and peers. Furthermore, it is pivotal to how students engage with learning content and relate to the learning environment itself. Despite the fact that communication theory (Vangelisti et al, 2013) offers a substantive basis for considering interpersonal exchanges in education, the introduction of technologies adds a degree of complexity and brings with it a number of unknowns. In this respect, it is misguided to think that technology in itself is the answer to effective communication. The hindrances and barriers to communication that existed prior to digitisation are most likely to continue to occur, whether using technologies or not. For this reason, the introduction of digital communication mediums requires additional thought. That being said, technologies offer exciting and dynamic ways of supporting and securing engagement. Their reach and range can demolish geographic boundaries and they have the potential, if used from an informed position, to reduce isolation and exclusion on a previously unimagined scale. In terms of expanding our understandings and navigating pedagogic change, it is the sharing of practice methods that we have found to be incredibly helpful.

The LearningWheel model, through its distinctive design, offers educators the opportunity to communicate the what, how and why of their technology usage in practice. Collaborators from across the profession are sought through the LearningWheel Twitter feed @LearningWheel and communication is supported by the use of the #learningwheel hashtag.

The @LearningWheel is a visual model of digital pedagogy with content created by teachers for teachers #learningwheel. https://twitter.com/learningwheel

This growing VCoL&P retweet and share tweeted information to generate interest and content. Technology-engaged educators provide examples from practice that are collated on a GoogleDoc (Figure 2.1) outlining the digital resources they use, how they use them and a rationale for why they use them. These contributions are curated by the LearningWheel team to form content that will eventually become the 'spokes' (Figure 1.2), which in total make up a LearningWheel. The LearningWheel we highlight in this section of the book was commissioned by the educational technology conference, 'Bett' (2016), to capture a picture of the digital methods and resources being used by educators to engage learners across the sector at that time. The visual presented in Figure 2.2 is an illustration of the communication mode engagement, taken from the completed LearningWheel (Kellsey, 2016a), that was curated from the collated suggestions of delegates who connected with this conference. It provides insights into the wide range of resources being used to support, secure and enhance methods of teaching for learning in the digital age. It is populated with digital resources and strategies that have been tried and tested by educators for educators. On first posting to the GoogleDoc, contributions might look something like the one on line 12 where the contributor has posted, *'Curate (subject) themed Scoop.It! articles and share across your social networks. Embed in VLE'* (Figure 2.1).

COMMUNICATION

Practitioners/Educators add your suggestions for using digital resources eg Dragon Dicitation, LinkedIn, Twitter, Skype, Yammer... to COMMUNICATE (any platform) with your Learners/Clients

Keep it short - keep it within the restraints of the box eg. 1 line/80 characters max

1 Curate **TWITTER** communications using **STORIFY.**

2 Use hashtag on **TWITTER** for short snippets for student information

3 **GOOGLEHangouts** to teach/discuss different study skills e.g. How to Harv ref.

4 Create **AR** triggers using book covers and link video reviews and key info

5 Create screencasts and explanations using **Screencast-o-Matic**

6 Hear all about it from @[subject]

7 Use **EXPLAINEVERYTHING** to make dynamic screencasts

8 Lost for words? WordFlex **TOUCH DICTATION** app to the rescue! Use for visual, interactive word-maps.

9 **DRAGON DICTATION** app allows students to use speech to text

10 Connect with like-minded people by writing about your interests on **WORDPRESS.**

11 Publish your research, thoughts, projects on **ISSUU.**

12 Curate [subject] themed **SCOOPIT!** articles. Share across your social networks. Embed in VLE.

13 Bring all comms together with private groups on **SLACK.**

14 Use 'private' social network **YAMMER** as a college, course, group, project communication tool

15 Read the latest [subject] chatter on the #[subject]chat on **TWITTER.**

16 If you can't meet face-2-face schedule a meeting/tutorial via **JOIN.ME**

17 **SKITCH** Get your point across with fewer words using annotation, shapes and sketches.

Figure 2.1 The Bett 2016 LearningWheel. Communication mode content GoogleDoc.

> The Bett 2016 LearningWheel. How do you use technology to engage with your students? Communication mode content GoogleDoc.
>
> https://docs.google.com/spreadsheets/d/1c0gNEaHw2M-fpDNVgTTK3BwQS 1Oef3KxZseiJZHH7qE/edit#gid=2134954465 (Kellsey, 2016).

Once curated, however, the same contribution will look something like this, *'Use Scoop.It! to curate subject specific content and share'* (see Figure 2.2).

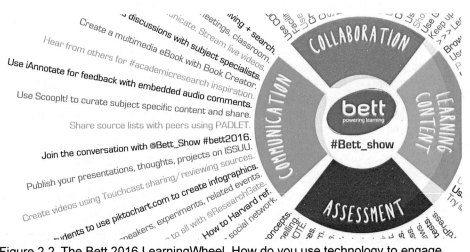

Figure 2.2 The Bett 2016 LearningWheel. How do you use technology to engage with your students?

> The Bett Show 2016 LearningWheel: How do you use technology to engage with your students? http://learningwheel.co.uk/2016/05/resource-lw/ (Kellsey, 2016a).

Here, as you can see, the educator has explained *what* is being used, in this instance 'Scoop.It!', *how* it is being used, 'to curate content' and *why* it is being used, to 'share' subject-specific information, which therefore aligns with the 'Ccommunication' mode of engagement (Figure 2.2). For those not familiar with Scoop.It! it is a web-based platform in a magazine format that is used mainly, but not solely, for collating, curating and sharing content on a particular theme or themes. Each of the authors have created and curated a Scoop.It! magazine in their respective areas of practice. The first author curates this magazine (www.scoop.it/t/learningwheel; Kellsey, 2013) to communicate resources that support the development of knowledge about the use of technologies for teachers and students across the further education sector. The second author has created and curates www.scoop.it/t/the-digital-social-worker (Taylor, 2016) to communicate to social work students, practitioners and fellow academics resources that will further inform the development of their technological knowledge and skills for practice. As a result of modelling usage, social work students have been enabled to develop the skills to curate and create subject-specific magazines which are linked to learning outcomes and summatively assessed as part of a module of learning. This learning activity is multilayered and creates an environment where the learner has the opportunity to engage with higher-order thinking skills (Krathwohl, 2002). Scoop.It! is just one example of a really useful and flexible platform that facilitates the curating, collating and communicating of content to a range of audiences, for different purposes. For educators who have not, as yet, used platforms such as Scoop.It! it might be that exploring the work of colleagues provides you with the confidence and motivation to do so.

We continue in this collaborative vein by again offering readers the opportunity to engage with the LearningWheel methodology, through making a contribution to the communication mode of engagement that can be found at the link below. Contributions to this mode of the LearningWheel should make reference to the digital tools and resources that have been used in practice to communicate and engage with students for a particular purpose. For clarity, we ask that when making suggestions colleagues outline *what* was used, *how* it was used and *why* it was used. The contributions made, as noted in the last chapter, will eventually become the 'LearningWheel Book: Top Apps and Resources' wheel generated by the readers of this book, which again we will share once we have the number of contributions required, across all four modes of engagement, to curate content.

LearningWheel Book: Top Apps and Resources

https://docs.google.com/spreadsheets/d/1EDRN4UaR6m93B_YEMGTZ8 EOISIWnfWsENkcDByWtWIM/edit#gid=2134954465 (Kellsey and Taylor, 2016).

To date, there have been some really interesting contributions to the LearningWheel VCoL&P that demonstrate how higher-order thinking skills can be made accessible when blended communication methods are applied. These are methods that move learners beyond more basic learning to activities that involve analysing, evaluating and creating (Diacopoulos, 2015). A really clear and accessible example is found in the work of Hayden (2016) who as a result of critiquing teaching methods, chose to supplement traditional approaches with the social media app Periscope (*what*) to live stream lectures (*how*) so that students could revisit learning content for revision purposes (*why*). Notable here is the way that this local teaching event, through the introduction of social media tools, morphed into a global classroom, where engagement with the subject matter became even more meaningful and to a degree applied (Hayden, 2016, slides 15–22). Students were not only enabled to theoretically explore the topic with the educator within the confines of their classroom but to do so through conversing with peers in a classroom in the US. In addition, the considered use of a subject-specific Twitter hashtag #ATOdebate facilitated and encouraged both synchronous and asynchronous communication. Here we can see the affordances of social media technologies in action. This carefully constructed blended approach extended the learning potential of the teaching event way beyond what traditional teaching methods could ever achieve. More importantly, this practice example illustrates that regardless of how technologies evolve, the critical, creative and progressive thinking of the teacher is crucial to education being 'affective' as well as 'effective'. This, in our opinion, is an example of blended learning (Kerres and Witt, 2003) at its best!

There are many other digital resources that can be used to communicate content, to connect learners and to co-produce knowledge. Alongside the diverse nature of these technologies is a distinct flexibility, that when married with scalability can be exploited in a manner that promotes communication which is not limited to place, space or time. This, of course, means that we need to move away from the discourse that indiscriminately separates the online from the offline, sometimes referred to as *'digital dualism'* (Jurgenson, 2012, p 83). We cannot afford to polarise virtual and face-to-face communications, favouring one over the other, due to the fact that it is through 'both' that our realities are now being created, recreated and where often our connections are made and maintained (Goffman, 1986; Rettie, 2004). Again, all of this comes back to educators thinking critically about the use of technologies as part of the overall pedagogic approach. It involves understanding that the term *'digital native'* (Prensky, 2001) is a less than accurate proposition to rely upon when thinking about effective and appropriate communication in education. We need to further consider the range of communication modes and mediums open to students and examine how these experiences are influencing and shaping the way in which learners learn. More importantly, we then need to exploit those technologies available in a way that complements and develops the potential for learning within the teaching space.

Our thinking about communication began with securing an understanding of the construct of the self and how this self is moulded and relational in the social world. It is with this type of relationality that we move on into the next chapter.

REFERENCES

Alimisis, D and Kynigos, C (2009) Constructionism and Robotics in Education, in D Alimisis (ed) *Teacher Education on Robotic-Enhanced Constructivist Pedagogical Methods*, pp 11–26. Athens: School of Pedagogical and Technological Education.

Attewell, J (2005) *Mobile Technologies and Learning*. London: Learning and Skills Development Agency.

Beckingham, S (2015) What Does It Mean To Be a Digital Lifewide Learner? *The Journal of Technology Enhanced Learning, Innovation and Change*, 1(1).

Benedictus, L (2016) Man v machine: Can computers cook, write and paint better than us? *The Guardian*. [online] Available at: www.theguardian.com/technology/2016/jun/04/man-v-machine-robots-artificial-intelligence-cook-write (accessed 12 August 2016).

Bett Show (2016) The world's leading education technology event. [online] Available at: www.bettshow.com/Content/About-Bett-Show (accessed 17 August 2016).

Blackwood, N (2016) Digital Skills Crisis: Second Report of Session 2016–17. Report, together with formal minutes relating to the report ordered by the House of Commons. [online] Available at: http://dera.ioe.ac.uk/26605/1/270.pdf (accessed 24 August 2016).

Blin, F and Munro, M (2008) Why Hasn't Technology Disrupted Academics' Teaching Practices? Understanding Resistance to Change through the Lens of Activity Theory. *Computers & Education*, 50(2): 475–90.

Bronfenbrenner, U (2009) *The Ecology of Human Development: Experiments by Nature and Design*. Cambridge, MA: Harvard University Press.

Bullard, J (2011) How the Use of Technology Enhances Children's Development. [online] Available at: www.johnpauliihs.org/wp/pattiweinbrenner/files/2011/11/Print-Education-uses-of-technology1.pdf (accessed 17 August 2016).

Costa, C (2014) The Habitus of Digital Scholars. *Research in Learning Technology*, 21. [online] Available at: www.researchinlearningtechnology.net/index.php/rlt/article/view/21274 (accessed 21 July 2016).

Cotter, E (2015) Teens and tech: What happens when students give up smartphones? *The Guardian*. [online] Available at: www.theguardian.com/teacher-network/2015/apr/23/teens-tech-students-give-up-smartphones (accessed 14 August 2016).

Dansieh, S A (2011) SMS Texting and Its Potential Impacts on Students' Written Communication Skills. *International Journal of English Linguistics*, 1(2): 222–29.

Diacopoulos, M M (2015) Untangling Web 2.0: Charting Web 2.0 Tools, the NCSS Guidelines for Effective Use of Technology, and Bloom's Taxonomy. *The Social Studies*, 106(4): 139–48.

Garrison, D R and Vaughan, N D (2008) *Blended Learning in Higher Education: Framework, Principles, and Guidelines*. San Francisco, CA: Jossey-Bass.

Goffman, E (1986) *Frame Analysis: An Essay on the Organization of Experience*. New York: Harper-Row.

Hanson, R (2016) *The Age of Em*. Oxford: Oxford University Press.

Hargie, O and Dickson, D (2004) *Skilled Interpersonal Communication*. 4th ed. London: Routledge.

Hayden, S (2016) How SOCIAL MEDIA can be used to enhance student's EMPLOYABILITY. [PowerPoint]. [online] Available at: https://docs.google.com/presentation/d/1Ki9JtJUY5j1xkMpN9hPnHcXBEXVO7IKEj_UAobZbHNA/edit?pref=2&pli=1#slide=id.p (accessed 23 August 2016).

Hennessy, S, Ruthven, K and Brindley, S (2005) Teacher Perspectives on Integrating ICT into Subject Teaching: Commitment, Constraints, Caution, and Change. *Journal of Curriculum Studies*, 37(2): 155–92.

Instefjord, E and Munthe, E (2016) Preparing Pre-service Teachers to Integrate Technology: An Analysis of the Emphasis on Digital Competence in Teacher Education Curricula. *European Journal of Teacher Education*, 39(1): 77–93.

Jurgenson, N (2012) When Atoms Meet Bits: Social Media, the Mobile Web and Augmented Revolution. *Future Internet*, 4(1): 83–91.

Kellsey, D (2013) The LearningWheel Scoop.It! [online] Available at: www.scoop.it/t/learningwheel (accessed 5 August 2016).

Kellsey, D (2016a) The Bett Show 2016 LearningWheel: How do you use technology to engage with your students? [online] Available at: http://learningwheel.co.uk/2016/05/resource-lw/ (accessed 27 July 2016).

Kellsey, D (2016b) The LearningWheel [website]. Available at: http://learningwheel.co.uk/ (accessed 28 August 2016).

Kellsey, D and Taylor, A M L (2016) LearningWheel Book: Top Apps and Resources. [online] Available at: https://docs.google.com/spreadsheets/d/1EDRN4UaR6m93B_YEMGTZ8EOISIWnfWsENkcDByWtWIM/edit#gid=2134954465 (accessed 30 August 2016).

Kerres, M and Witt, C D (2003) A Didactical Framework for the Design of Blended Learning Arrangements. *Journal of Educational Media*, 28(2–3): 101–13.

Khanna, P (2016) *Connectography: Mapping the Future of Global Civilization*. New York: Random House Books.

Kolowich, S (2011) How Will Students Communicate? *Inside Higher Ed*, 6. [online] Available at: www.insidehighered.com/news/2011/01/06/college_technology_officers_consider_changing_norms_in_student_communications (accessed 16 November 2016).

Krathwohl, D R (2002) A Revision of Bloom's Taxonomy: An Overview. *Theory into Practice*, 41(4): 212–18.

Mathers, M B (2016) #FELTAG revisited … The BOBSTED Report: A visual conversation with @bobharrisonset @cityandguilds. @BryanMMathers [Twitter] 1 August 2016. [online] Available at: https://twitter.com/BryanMMathers/status/760126204221337601 (accessed 3 August 2016).

Myers, T S, Blackman, A, Andersen, T, Hay, R, Lee, I and Gray, H (2014) Cultivating ICT Students' Interpersonal Soft Skills in Online Learning Environments Using Traditional Active Learning Techniques. *Journal of Learning Design*, 7(3): 39–53.

Ofcom (2016) The Communications Market Report 2016. [online] Available at: http://stakeholders.ofcom.org.uk/binaries/research/cmr/cmr16/uk/CMR_UK_2016.pdf (accessed 24 August 2016).

Patterson, L, Carrillo, P B and Salinas, R S (2011) Lessons from a Global Learning Virtual Classroom. *Journal of Studies in International Education*, 16(20): 182–97.

Prensky, M (2001) Digital Natives, Digital Immigrants: Part 1. *On the Horizon*, 9(5): 1–6.

Przybylski, A K and Weinstein, N (2013) Can You Connect with Me Now? How the Presence of Mobile Communication Technology Influences Face-To-Face Conversation Quality. *Journal of Social and Personal Relationships*, 30(3): 237–46.

Ravizza, S M, Hambrick, D Z and Fenn, K M (2014) Non-Academic Internet Use in the Classroom is Negatively Related to Classroom Learning Regardless of Intellectual Ability. *Computers & Education*, 78: 109–14.

Rettie, R (2004). Using Goffman's Frameworks to Explain Presence and Reality. *Presence 2004: Seventh Annual International Workshop*, pp 117–24. Valencia: ISPR.

Rogers, B (2015) *Classroom Behaviour: A Practical Guide to Effective Teaching, Behaviour Management and Colleague Support*. London: Sage.

Rogers, C R (1957) The Necessary and Sufficient Conditions of Therapeutic Personality Change. *Journal of Consulting Psychology*, 21(2): 95–103.

Stein, J L (1996) Ideology and the Telephone: The Social Reception of a Technology. London 1876–1920. Doctoral dissertation, University of London.

Stephens, K K and Pantoja, G E (2016) Mobile Devices in the Classroom: Learning Motivations Predict Specific Types of Multicommunicating Behaviors. *Communication Education*, 1(17): 463–79.

Susskind, R E and Susskind, D (2015) *The Future of the Professions: How Technology Will Transform the Work of Human Experts*. Oxford: Open University Press.

Taylor, A M L (2016) The Digital Social Worker Scoop.It! [online] Available at: www.scoop.it/t/the-digital-social-worker (accessed 5 August 2016).

Turkle, S (2015) *Reclaiming Conversation: The Power of Talk in a Digital Age*. New York: Penguin Press.

Vangelisti, A L, Daly, J A and Friedrich, G W (2013) *Teaching Communication: Theory, Research, and Methods.* Abingdon, Oxon: Routledge.

Warschauer, M (2001) Online Communication, in Carter, R and Nunan, D (eds) *The Cambridge Guide to Teaching English to Speakers of Other Languages*, pp 207–12. Cambridge: Cambridge University Press.

Watson, D M (2001) Pedagogy before Technology: Re-thinking the Relationship between ICT and Teaching. *Education and Information Technologies*, 6(4): 251–66.

Wenger, E (2014) *Artificial Intelligence and Tutoring Systems: Computational and Cognitive Approaches to the Communication of Knowledge.* Los Altos, CA: Morgan Kaufmann.

Young, M and Muller, J (2010) Three Educational Scenarios for the Future: Lessons from the Sociology of Knowledge. *European Journal of Education*, 45(1): 11–27.

Connected or confined?

Collaboration is not new to educators or education; indeed, collaborative pedagogy has historically been, and remains, central to thinking about how students learn (De Hei et al, 2015). As a teaching approach, it promotes participation and encourages contribution, alongside facilitating the occasion to co-produce knowledge. It naturally stimulates individual, group and task appraisal and as a learning experience has the potential to generate the types of feedback that can engender critical thinking, and that can develop a range of *'soft skills'* (Chamorro-Premuzic et al, 2007, p 221). In general terms, it would take the form of small groupwork that might involve activities such as project-based tasks, simulation, debates, problem-solving or creative endeavours. These are learning events where learners would be encouraged to learn what it means to work in groups in a participatory and cohesive manner, and more particularly to learn with and from each other (Vygotsky, 1978). Before modern technologies in their current form began to penetrate education, collaboration was a much more local-type affair (Weindling, 2005). Student networks were predominantly limited to the confines of the physical classroom, immediate peer groups, and a designated educator; all of which would be largely enclosed within the walls of the attending institution. Various methods would be employed in an attempt to expose students to wider networks but these principally relied upon individual teacher knowledge and industry connections and were often hindered by logistics, finance and competing demands on time (Lortie, 1975). All of this was prior to digitisation and an understanding of the possibilities that technologies and blended approaches afford, and it was not only the student experience that was limited. Teachers themselves, by the very nature of the education structures, experienced restrictions with regards to access to the wider teaching community, and therefore the opportunities and benefits that lie therein (Stoll et al, 2006). The rise of the highly populated @UKEdChat Community of Learning and practice, which is principally maintained on the social media platform Twitter using the hashtag #UKEdChat, evidences the very real need for mediums that facilitate collaboration in education (UKEdChat, 2010).

CRITICAL **REFLECTION**

Thinking about collaboration, we ask you to reflect upon ...

- *the methods you use to facilitate collaborative learning and those you employ to assist students in developing their networks?*
- *how would you define yourself as an educator ... connected or confined or somewhere in the middle of the two?*

As explained in the introduction to this text, the LearningWheel model was devised as a means of appraising digital practices, an aid to the development of blended learning methods and also a context in which to evaluate the inclusion and subsequent coherence of technology-enhanced teaching approaches. In addition, it was designed to generate a Community of Learning, with the emphasis being on that of collaborative contributions. The LearningWheel model relies heavily upon collaborative practice due to its community orientation. Without contributions from educators and learning technologists the LearningWheel as a digital resource would be devoid of content and therefore purpose, because as Salmon (2013) points out, for collaboration in education to be meaningful it requires the *'active sharing of information and intellectual resources'* (p 144). Inherent in the model are features that present educators with authentic opportunities to model technology-enhanced collaboration, and furthermore to purposively demonstrate those technologies relevant to the development of digital capabilities for learners of the connected age (JISC, 2015). The latter presents a tangible opportunity to attend to the findings of Littlejohn et al (2012), who urge institutions *'to place greater value on "literacies of the digital", and better prepare students ... for future challenges'* (p 554). In addition, its accessibility and the way in which it strengthens the potential for the cross-fertilisation of knowledge means that it is also a context in which genuine collaboration can be fostered. While each mode of engagement has its own distinct set of characteristics, it is the collaboration mode that is key to using the LearningWheel in its fullness as a pedagogic approach. In fact, the most effective examples of digital pedagogy contributed to the LearningWheel (Kellsey, 2016) thus far evidence a balance in the weight of attention paid to each of the modes of engagement.

Like the other modes of engagement, this mode encourages teacher to teacher, teacher to student, student to student (Cardak and Selvi, 2016), and student to employer collaboration, with the intention of illustrating how said collaboration, in the age of digitisation, no longer needs to be confined to local or institutional networks. Hence this is why we have developed the 'The CoActED Learner' graphic (Figure 3.1). This is a visual mapping tool, and is designed to complement the more traditional approaches that educators employ when prompting learners to reflect upon and build their networks. 'Co' represents connection and collaboration, with 'Act' pointing towards activity and action between the potential actors involved within the network, and 'ED' indicating the purpose – to support the educative process. The CoActED tool, as a byproduct of the LearningWheel innovation, allows learners, and educators themselves, to consider the idea of networks and networking, and to reflect upon the skills required to collaborate. Each of the labelled circles prompts students to identify actual and possible networks and communities relevant to their development, be that a peer, a learning community, an academic community, an industry, an employer or a community of peers, locally or globally, with the view to them acting upon any gaps they might find. The result is a map of connections; those established, those being made, and those that could complement a learning journey in its totality (Warschauer et al, 1996).

THE LEARNINGWHEEL
The CoActED Learner   www.learningwheel.co.uk

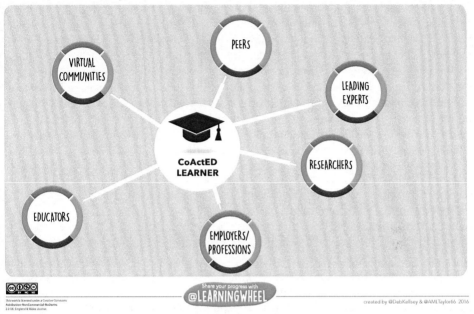

Figure 3.1 The CoActED Learner (Taylor and Kellsey, 2016).

The CoActED Learner http://learningwheel.co.uk/call-coacted-learner-maps/
(Taylor and Kellsey, 2016a)

CRITICAL **REFLECTION**

Thinking about collaboration and networks, we invite you to …

- *map your professional network on the CoActED visual (Figure 3.1) and submit it on the LearningWheel website: http://learningwheel.co.uk/call-coacted-learner-maps/.*

Another recent addition to the LearningWheel methodology, and our response to a more targeted approach to CPD and networking for educators and practitioners, is that of the Conference LearningWheel (Taylor and Kellsey, 2016). The Conference LearningWheel design builds upon the original LearningWheel model in that it aims to capture technology usage within a particular Community of Learning or practice, while sharing the collated and curated content more widely throughout the community in question. Conferences before the connected age occurred in a particular space, at a particular time, with a particular audience. The construct of the conference meant that only the delegates in attendance could hear from and interact with the experts in that field about new innovations and emerging knowledge relating to the practice of that professional grouping. Delegates would leave the space having had their thinking influenced, shaped or perhaps even challenged, and it would be expected that they would be the vehicles of knowledge transfer for non-attending practice colleagues. Technological developments have changed all of that (Jacobs and McFarlane, 2005), and we now have live-streamed conference presentations, the microblogging of presenters' content via platforms such as Twitter (Ross et al, 2011) and the sharing of academic papers on various other social media sites. Our idea aims to draw conference content into a single space, and as you will see by clicking on the link below, in addition to the more standard LearningWheel graphic, we have made use of Quick Response (QR) codes to achieve this.

> The Conference Wheel http://learningwheel.co.uk/about-learningwheel/conference-learningwheel/ (Taylor and Kellsey, 2016).

It could be argued that the Conference LearningWheel merely offers information that ordinarily would be found and accessed on a conference website. However, the way in which the tool condenses content means that not only does it capture the essence of the conference but it does so in a way that is more likely to keep the conversation going and add life to the material post the event. In relation to collaboration, what is even more interesting about this method of curating and collating conference content is that delegates are offered a further occasion to actively participate. The opportunity to shape and inform conference content comes in the form of 'spoke' suggestions (Figure 1.2) alongside adding content to a designated hashtag. It goes without saying that content sharing practices should be underpinned by an understanding of intellectual property, copyright and the more general rules around the distribution of content. We believe this method of facilitating CPD for educators and practitioners to add to the many other creative methods being developed by innovators in our midst.

A call to collaborate

Undeniable is the fact that there is much more learning to be had from learning together as opposed to learning alone. Where there is collaboration there is a group, and where there is a group in education there is a need for the application of groupwork theory (Brown, 1988; Douglas, 2002; Lewin, 1943). An understanding of the complex dynamics that groups can arouse, which can be further amplified or complicated when groups engage online (Goulet et al, 2003; Nitsun, 2014), is fundamental to facilitating a group and consequently to how successful that group will be (Schmuck and Schmuck, 1975). In Chapter 2 we outlined how, through the informed and effective use of communication technologies, collaboration can be made even more possible. Here we highlight the importance of skilled interpersonal communication for collaborating effectively within a group, particularly when online, as the nuances of face-to-face communication are less available to the messenger and the receiver (Curtis and Lawson, 2001). Given the various forms that online communication takes and how this type of communication is largely perceived (Resnyansky, 2009), applying groupwork theory is essential to the construction of collaborative learning spaces. The shifts that can transpire in relation to group dynamics when communication is virtual (Graham, 2006) call for learning activities that have the potential to enable students to learn about and acquire the skill set necessary to navigate such interpersonal exchanges. Returning to interpersonal communication (Hargie et al, 1994) and groupwork theory (Benson, 2009) will provide educators with a lens through which they can consider the differences in the relational nature of online and offline groups (Ramirez and Zhang, 2007). This type of awareness will help to establish and maintain a group, while allowing for the modelling of appropriate interpersonal exchanges. Once educators, and subsequently, learners, acquire an understanding of the interplay between these two spaces, in terms of what each demands, then the group can progress and be perceived as a collaborative venture (Koh et al, 2009).

CRITICAL **REFLECTION**

Thinking about collaboration and groupwork, it would be useful to ...

- *consider how groupwork theory might be applied when collaborating in virtual spaces and the methods that could be employed to model effective online communication.*

There are a number of accessible online resources that can support the development and maintenance of collaboration in the form of *'learning communities'* (Stoll et al, 2006). These communities can be virtual groupings or groupings that meet in physical learning environments or both – a collective of learners that regularly or periodically meet for a common purpose, be that online, offline or both. For example, a Massive Open Online Course (MOOC) learning community might never meet in person but as a group engage in behaviours similar to learners who gather in a physical space (Harasim, 1995). Then there are the groupings that meet in physical spaces who might use technologies but only in a classroom environment. Alternatively, a truly blended approach would incorporate technologies strategically into actual and virtual teaching and learning spaces, aligning the teaching methodology with the learning outcomes. The point is that the groupings and the spaces in which they converge can be as diverse as the tools and resources employed to secure effective and purposive collaboration. However, what is important is that the tools or resources chosen for the purposes of collaboration are appropriate to the activity and that their usage is underpinned by pedagogy, and where relevant andragogy (Morgan and Adams, 2009). The 'Substitution Augmentation Modification Redefinition' (SAMR) model is an another incredibly useful framework to employ when thinking through the accuracy and appropriateness of the technology chosen and the approach taken (Puentedura, 2012). Educators engaged with the LearningWheel community have provided many examples of blended learning approaches, where collaboration was key to maximising the learning potential. A substantive example is found in the creative work of Kieft (2015), whose visual representation of technology usage can be seen in this engaging infographic: https://magic.piktochart.com/output/6179691-g-communites. Here, Kieft (2015) graphically illustrates the what, how and why of said usage. The *what* on this occasion is that of Google+, *how* to create an online discussion space, *why* for the purposes of curating subject-specific content, generating engagement, while affording students with the opportunity to become familiar with the skills pertinent to collaborating in online spaces. Another example, this time from the higher education sector, comes in the form of a Book Group (Taylor, 2015). Figure 3.2 outlines the methodology.

Social Work Book Group

Social Work Book Group is an actual and virtual Community of Learning that meets quarterly to discuss a book chosen by students. The text selected is a piece of fiction that students deem to be relevant to their studies. The book chosen must include characters and sociological conditions that are relatable to social work practice. Often there will be eight to ten university-based Book Groups engaging simultaneously. Each of the universities involved with the project will host an event. This includes taking responsibility for choosing the book, outlining the text and the themes arising, and communicating this information through the use of a streaming technology. An electronic link to the streaming technology is circulated on Twitter. This enables the learning community to visually connect and to communicate in relation to the identified themes that provide a context for the discussion.

Each of the student groups tunes into the live stream, having read and annotated the text using a method called dialectical journaling (Taylor, 2015) to connect with the fictive content. Communication and engagement are further facilitated through the group Twitter feed @SWBookGroup using the hashtag #swbk. Once the themes for the discussion are established, each of the groups in their respective institutions engage in a separate discussion while simultaneously communicating on Twitter to broaden the discussion further. The hashtag is used as a tool to connect, collate and continue the conversation. Incorporating these methods of connecting students to the collaborative process maximises the learning that can be gained from this global classroom.

Students who are unable to physically attend the group can engage with it virtually. The flexibility that the construct of the learning activity offers promotes collaboration and inclusion, with the digital resources providing access and engagement pre, during and post the event. This teaching and learning methodology has been adopted internationally and by a wide range of disciplines including medicine, nursing and psychiatry.

A chronology of each of the Book Group events can be accessed via this link: https://storify.com/AMLTaylor66/the-use-of-book-clubs-in-social-work-education (Taylor, 2013).

Figure 3.2 Social Work Book Group case study (Taylor, 2013).

This case study, as you can see, provides an example of a collaborative learning community that is both local and global. This group meet with the collective purpose (Doel and Sawdon, 1999) of engaging in critical reflection aligned to curriculum content, with the aim of consolidating understandings across the programme of study. It is a blended learning methodology that can be applied across the range of subject areas and can be adapted to meet the needs of a particular learning group. Furthermore, it is synchronous or asynchronous (Hrastinski, 2008) in that engagement can be online and offline, separately or at the same time. In short, it is a diverse teaching and learning approach (Knight et al, 2015), enhanced by the use of technologies to create a space that can and does among other things offer access to peer support while facilitating knowledge acquisition. The *what* is Twitter and Periscope, the *how* is to establish communication channels and record learning content, while the *why* is to connect learners in a collaborative process linked to curriculum content that aims to provide them with the opportunity to consolidate knowledge and to explore digital professionalism for practice.

These types of actual and virtual learning spaces are not totally unique in terms of access to learning or resources given that increasingly university libraries are extending their opening hours to 24 hours a day seven days a week. However, what is unique is that access is not geographically restricted, engagement can be instantaneous, directed by the learner and much richer in terms of the abundance and breadth of content made available. Furthermore, they illustrate that the classroom is now everywhere and anywhere (Jung and Latchem, 2011), and at times it might be that it is positioned as such for a particular learning purpose. Additional examples of blended approaches for the purposes of collaboration, shared from within the LearningWheel VCoL&P (Figure 3.3), further illustrate the ways in which technologies are being integrated into educational processes. The LearningWheel being referred to here was commissioned by a small group of librarians from a further education institution who, due to a notable increase in student engagement as a result of embedding technologies into approaches, were keen to connect with the wider librarian community to exchange methods. The result was 'The Library Skills & Research Subject LearningWheel' (Kellsey, 2015) populated by librarians for librarians. This was a collaborative process that led to the sharing of a range of evidence-based practices that were found to impact positively upon the students' library habits and subsequent learning journey. As can be seen in Figure 3.3, the technologies were purposively chosen and skillfully employed to encourage interaction with specific library resources that can support learning. Additionally, digital resources were also deployed in a manner that encouraged student–librarian collaboration aimed at shaping library content and purposes. One such technology being used was that of Padlet, a versatile online platform that is becoming increasingly popular within the education context to curate content for group discussion, to collaborate on projects and assess engagement. On this occasion, the *what* is Padlet, which is embedded into the institutional library VLE space, this action equating to the *how*, as a means to engage students with the development of library resources, the *why* of the overall process. Another submitted practice example describes the use of Periscope and Twitter, the *what*, to record library tours, the *how*, with the *why* being the intentional sharing of information with students for the purposes of orientation. Learning content was further delivered through the opportunity to engage in an online discussion with library staff.

47

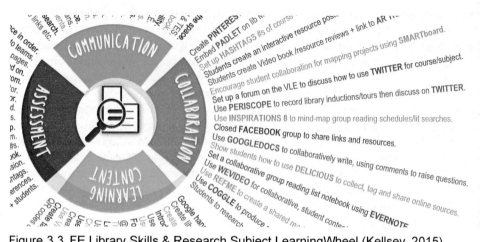

Figure 3.3 FE Library Skills & Research Subject LearningWheel (Kellsey, 2015).

FE Library Skills & Research Subject LearningWheel http://learningwheel.co.uk/2016/06/fe-library-skills-research/ (Kellsey, 2015)

The collaborative content of this LearningWheel is innovative, diverse, engaging and purposive. It highlights the educational values of partnership, inclusion and reflective practice (SEDA, nd) and furthermore is progressive in nature. It illustrates the potential to release the knowledge within a learning community to effect change and through its online presence promotes inclusivity on a much wider scale.

As Salmon (2013, p 145) reminds us:

one of the best ways of encouraging collaboration is around a highly invitational group task.

The LearningWheel offers educators the opportunity to share digital practice and methods within a lively and dynamic network. The invitation is an open one, but the benefits can only be felt once the process has been engaged with. It is therefore in this vein that we once again invite readers to join us in a collaborative venture, one that has been made accessible through the link below. It is a call to collaborate, to the Top Apps and Resources LearningWheel, that we hope to create through the readership of this book. Contributions again should outline the *what*, the *how* and the *why* of the digital resource used for the purposes of collaboration within the education context, and shared with the aim of generating further creativity in the use of technologies that can enhance practice across the sector.

LearningWheel Book: Top Apps and Resources

https://drive.google.com/open?id=1EDRN4UaR6m93B_YEMGTZ8EOISI WnfWsENkcDByWtWlM (Kellsey and Taylor, 2016b).

Fundamentally, collaboration is about people and human interaction. There is little doubt that technologies can, and do 'enhance' educational processes and practice. As educators, however, it is important that we hold on to the human-first element of digital practices, be that in terms of purpose, function or outputs. Technologies, throughout our existence, have been developed to progress society more broadly (Castells, 2010), but lest we forget these developments have been the work of humans ... for humans. The current discourse around digitisation in many ways appears to separate and negate human involvement in the process. Holding on to a view that celebrates our developments, our technological advancements and our successes as humans feels like a much more collaborative and rational stance in what can at times be a technology-first world. In the education context, it is the 'human' practitioner who creates and constructs 'human' experiences for those engaging with a 'human' system (Moore, 1993). Assessing the appropriateness of technologies in education is an ethical privilege as well as a professional judgement. This assessment, as we alluded to earlier in the book, starts with an appraisal of the professional self, because without this the effectiveness of any approach taken is immediately undermined. It is with this thought that we proceed to Chapter 4, where we discuss the 'assessment' mode of engagement.

REFERENCES

Benson, J (2009) *Working More Creatively with Groups*. 3rd ed. London: Routledge.

Brown, R J (1988) *Group Processes: Dynamics within and between Groups*. Oxford: Blackwell.

Cardak, C S and Selvi, K (2016) Increasing Teacher Candidates' Ways of Interaction and Levels of Learning through Action Research in a Blended Course. *Computers in Human Behavior*, 61: 488–506.

Castells, M. (2010) *The Rise of the Network Society: The Information Age: Economy, Society, and Culture*. Oxford: Blackwell Publishers.

Chamorro-Premuzic, T, Furnham, A and Lewis, M (2007) Personality and Approaches to Learning Predict Preference for Different Teaching Methods. *Learning and Individual Differences* 17(3): 241–50.

Curtis, D D and Lawson, M J (2001) Exploring Collaborative Online Learning. *Journal of Asynchronous Learning Networks*, 5(1): 21–34.

De Hei, M S A, Strijbos, J W, Sjoer, E and Admiraal, W (2015) Collaborative Learning in Higher Education: Lecturers' Practices and Beliefs. *Research Papers in Education*, 30(2): 232–47.

Doel, M and Sawdon, C (1999) *The Essential Groupworker: Teaching and Learning Creative Groupwork*. London: Jessica Kingsley Publishers.

Douglas, T (2002). *Basic Groupwork*. London: Routledge.

Goulet, L, Krentz, C and Christiansen, H (2003) Collaboration in Education: The Phenomenon and Process of Working Together. *Alberta Journal of Educational Research*, 49(4): 325–40.

Graham, C R (2006) Blended Learning Systems: Definition, Current Trends, and Future Directions, in C J Bonk and C R Graham (eds) *Handbook of Blended Learning: Global Perspectives, Local Designs*, pp 3–21. San Francisco, CA: Pfeiffer Publishing.

Harasim, L (1995) Online Education: The Future, in Harrison, T M and Stephen, T D (eds) *Computer Networking and Scholarly Communication in the Twenty-First-Century University*, pp 203–14. New York: SUNY Press.

Hargie, O, Saunders, C and Dickson, D (1994) *Social Skills in Interpersonal Communication*. London: Routledge.

Hrastinski, S (2008) Asynchronous and Synchronous E-Learning. *Educause Quarterly*, 31(4): 51–5.

Jacobs, N and McFarlane, A (2005) Conferences as Learning Communities: Some Early Lessons in Using 'Back-channel' Technologies at an Academic Conference – Distributed Intelligence or Divided Attention? *Journal of Computer Assisted Learning*, 21(5): 317–29.

JISC (2015) Developing students' digital literacy. [online] Available at: www.jisc.ac.uk/rd/projects/digital-literacies (accessed 15 September 2016).

Jung, I and Latchem, C (2011) A Model for E-Education: Extended Teaching Spaces and Extended Learning Spaces. *British Journal of Educational Technology*, 42(1): 6–18.

Kellsey, D (2015) FE Library Skills & Research Subject LearningWheel. [online] Available at: http://learningwheel.co.uk/2016/06/fe-library-skills-research/ (accessed 4 September 2016).

Kellsey, D (2016) The LearningWheel [website]. [online] Available at: http://learningwheel.co.uk/ (accessed 26 August 2016).

Kellsey, D and Taylor, A M L (2016) LearningWheel Book: Top Apps and Resources. [online] Available at: https://docs.google.com/spreadsheets/d/1EDRN4UaR6m93B_YEMGTZ8EOISIWnfWsENkcDByWtWIM/edit#gid=2134954465 (accessed 30 August, 2016).

Kieft, J (2015) G+ Communities: All you need to know [infographic]. [online] Available at: https://magic.piktochart.com/output/6179691-g-communites (accessed 1 September 2016).

Knight, S, Killen, C and Smith, R (2015) Using technology to improve curriculum design. [online] Available at: www.jisc.ac.uk/guides/using-technology-to-improve-curriculum-design (accessed 14 September 2016).

Koh, C, Wang, C J, Tan, O S, Liu, W C and Ee, J (2009) Bridging the Gaps between Students' Perceptions of Group Project Work and Their Teachers' Expectations. *The Journal of Educational Research*, 102(5): 333–48.

Lewin, K (1943) Psychology and the Process of Group Living. *The Journal of Social Psychology*, 17(1): 113–31.

Littlejohn, A, Beetham, H and McGill, L (2012) Learning at the Digital Frontier: A Review of Digital Literacies in Theory and Practice. *Journal of Computer Assisted Learning*, 28(6): 547–56.

Lortie, D (1975) *Schoolteacher: A Sociological Study*. Chicago: University of Chicago Press.

Moore, M (1993) Theory of Transactional Distance, in Keegan, D (ed) *Theoretical Principles of Distance Education*, pp 22–38. London: Routledge.

Morgan, G and Adams, J (2009) Pedagogy First: Making Web-technologies Work for Soft Skills Development in Leadership and Management Education. *Journal of Interactive Learning Research*, 20(2): 129–55.

Nitsun, M (2014) *The Anti-group: Destructive Forces in the Group and Their Creative Potential*. London: Routledge.

Puentedura, R R (2012) The SAMR model: Background and exemplars. [online] Available at: www.hippasus.com/rrpweblog/archives/000073.html (accessed 16 September 2016).

Ramirez Jr, A and Zhang, S (2007) When Online Meets Offline: The Effect of Modality Switching on Relational Communication. *Communication Monographs*, 74(3): 287–310.

Resnyansky, L (2009) Computer-mediated Communication in Higher Education: Educator's Agency in Relation to Technology. *The Journal of Educational Enquiry*, 3(1): 35–59.

Ross, C, Terras, M, Warwick, C and Welsh, A (2011) Enabled Backchannel: Conference Twitter Use by Digital Humanists. *Journal of Documentation*, 67(2): 214–37.

Salmon, G (2013) *E-tivities: The Key to Active Online Learning*. Oxon: Routledge.

Schmuck, R A and Schmuck, P A (1975). *Group Processes in the Classroom*. 8th ed. New York: McGraw Hill.

SEDA (nd) Core mission and values. [online] Available at: www.seda.ac.uk/core-mission-values (accessed 15 September 2016).

Stoll, L, Bolam, R, McMahon, A, Wallace, M and Thomas, S (2006) Professional Learning Communities: A Review of the Literature. *Journal of Educational Change*, 7(4): 221–58.

Taylor, A M L (2013) The use of book groups in social work education and practice. [online] Available at: https://storify.com/AMLTaylor66/the-use-of-book-clubs-in-social-work-education (accessed 10 September 2016).

Taylor, A M L (2015) When Actual Met Virtual, in Westwood, J (ed) *Social Media in Social Work Education*. Northwich, Cheshire: Critical Publishing.

Taylor, A M L and Kellsey, D. (2016a) The Conference Wheel. [online] Available at: http://learningwheel.co.uk/about-learningwheel/conference-learningwheel/ (accessed 2 September 2016).

Taylor, A M L and Kellsey, D (2016b) The CoActED learner maps. [online] Available at: http://learningwheel.co.uk/call-coacted-learner-maps/ (accessed 1 September 2016).

UKEdChat (2010) A community of teachers and educationalists: Focused on CPD, pedagogy & improving teaching. [Twitter]. [online] Available at: https://twitter.com/ukedchat (accessed 13 September 2016).

Vygotsky, L S (1978) *Mind in Society: The Development of Higher Psychological Processes*. Cambridge: Harvard University Press.

Warschauer, M, Turbee, L and Roberts, B (1996) Computer Learning Networks and Student Empowerment. *System*, 24(1): 1–14.

Weindling, D (2005) Teachers as Collaborative Professionals. [online] Available at: www.atl.org.uk/Images/Teachers%20as%20collaborative%20professionals.pdf (accessed 2 September 2016).

Actualising through assessment

If education is fundamental to self-actualisation, then as Race et al (2005, p xi) explain:

nothing we do to, or for our students is more important than our assessment of their work and the feedback we give them on it. [Because] the results of our assessment influence students for the rest of their lives …

Concerning therefore is the fact that assessment seems to be one of the most heavily contested, widely debated and highly misunderstood areas of academic practice there is (Boud and Molloy, 2013; Race, 2002). It is an educational concept that is surrounded by negativity, one that, more often than not, is met with suspicion and unease. Indeed, Taras (2005, p 469) discusses how *'the terrors evoked by the term "assessment" have distorted its necessity, centrality and its potentially neutral position'*. Even though *'assessment permeates every aspect of our lives, and is a natural and automatic activity'* (Rowntree, 1987, p 4), the attributed discourse and its usage within education somehow fails to fully reflect the complex variables involved. As an educational process, much depends upon assessment, and despite a substantial body of literature that evidences ongoing efforts to address and improve it (Astin, 2012; Boud, 2013; Falchikov, 2013; Race, 2014), the challenges persist. Boud and Molloy (2013, p 8) explain that even though research suggests the need to change assessment practices, there remains *'surprisingly little awareness of what needs to be done'*. Yet there is a significant amount of pressure to 'get it right', which is not only felt by students. Educators too are under increasing strain to evidence the impact of their work, through baseline measurements that are often reduced to student retention and academic success (Harris, 2015). These, and other similarly defined indicators of impact, have been instrumental in shaping the discourse, and subsequently how assessment is engaged with and perceived. An understanding of how assessment has become such a feared and at times misemployed method is therefore key to how we work to redress the balance, and in contemporary education technologies have a part to play. This is not to say that technologies are the answer. In fact, as Kirkwood and Price (2008, p 1) state, *'there is ample evidence of technology-led innovations failing to achieve the transformations expected by educators'*, and this is where the critical analysis of any digital resource chosen is crucial to its adoption.

Helpful for contemplating the nature of assessment is this claim from Gibbs (1999), who describes it as *'the most powerful lever teachers have to influence the way students respond to a course and behave as learners'* (p 41). Gibbs' comment implies that teachers are invested in efforts to maximise engagement and secure attainment, and indeed, without any shadow of doubt … they are. However, there are undertones in this assertion, a subtext of power and control, that reflect the uneasy tension that exists, relating not only to how assessment is used but also with regards to how it is understood. Boud's refreshingly forthright and appropriately challenging opinion on this is that *'assessment acts as a mechanism to control students that is far more pervasive and insidious than most staff would be prepared to acknowledge'* (Boud, 1995, p 35). Thinking about assessment in this, or similar ways inadvertently maintains the discourse of fear, and could in effect lead learners to disengage, and therefore underachieve. Kirkwood and Price's discussion regarding *'conceptions of learning'* (2008, p 3) is useful here given the importance of understanding learner socialisation and how this influences what learners understand learning to be. While they offer some interesting comments about how engagement with learning is influenced by conceptions of learning, they say less about the part institutional practices play in shaping learning behaviours. So, for example, if it is that students are being taught in environments that employ authoritarian approaches, ones that they introject as prescriptive, directive or largely constraining, it should come as no surprise that a large percentage of them find it difficult to engage and achieve (Boud, 1995). Although none of this is straightforward, as can been seen through the reflections of the philosopher Marshall Berman, in a newspaper article that questions the overarching ethos of the British education system (Dorling, 2014). Berman is quoted in this piece to have explained his education as *'intellectually exciting but socially lonely ... [in that it] catered to the rich, and to the current and wannabe ruling class'* – encounters that he describes to have left him feeling like he *'didn't fit in'* (Dorling, 2014, np). Inasmuch as Berman's experiences appear not to have had an impact upon his success, they highlight how assessment as an academic activity has a sociological context. So perhaps, as extreme as it might seem, Dorling (2014, np) is correct to believe that Britain has *'an educational system that is designed to polarise people, one that creates an elite'*. That being said, we have a slightly different view of education and a learner's experience of it, in that we see it as a predominantly subjective activity, immersed in institutional norms that do not always understand or prioritise what it is that students need.

It goes without saying that socialisation is not something that occurs entirely inside of the regime, and that each student comes to education with a psychosocial story of their own (Froggett, 2002). Nonetheless, educational experiences have a significant impact upon this, and self-actualisation (Schmeck, 1988) more broadly. They can mould learners into unhelpful ways of being that are difficult to undo. If, for example, a learner is assessed as not having achieved, or deemed to have underachieved, there are a complex set of meanings that can arise. We need to bear in mind that *'students do not ... share a similar understanding of academic discourse as the tutor'* (Weaver, 2006, p 380) and pay due consideration to how problematic unfiltered language can be. This is particularly the case if this involves *'judgmental statements'* that are perceived as *'critical or dismissive, [because it is these that] can cause anger or hurt'* (Weaver 2006, p 381). Feedback in this respect can be a *'troublesome'* (Meyer and Land, 2006) tool, in that it is largely fuelled by what is often unhelpful and inaccessible language (Court, 2014), which subsequently influences how a learner might re-engage with their learning post an assessment event. As Berman's account shows, these issues do not solely relate to those who may be labeled under- or non-achieving learners; they can raise issues for those deemed to be high-achieving students, as they too feel the pressures that educational processes can evoke (Falchikov, 2013).

Returning to Gibbs (1999), we agree that there is a need for motivational-type strategies that prompt and support achievement, and most certainly provide a place for rewarding efforts (Orsmond et al, 2005). We are not, however, convinced that the dominant narrative of assessment across education is helpful, in that it does little to promote engagement, or speak to the population of learners equally (Goodwin, 2012). Race (2002) in some of his earlier work suggests that *'assessment is broken'* (np); given how assessment appears to be thought about and used, we would question how it was ever thought of as 'fixed'? Finding Boud and Molloy (2013, p 3) over ten years later questioning the usefulness of *'instrumental band-aid solutions'* to the problems with assessment signals that not much has changed. While this is a subject much bigger than is possible to cover within the confines of this book, for now it is suffice to say that there are significant issues with assessment, and that these do not lie entirely in the hands of educators. Educational processes are driven by a wider political agenda, and manifest in complicated ways (Ingram and Waller, 2016), many of which are entrenched in negative notions of difference that are principally linked to achievement, power and class. Despite all of this, we as educators have a role to play, and a responsibility to understand the learner in context. Therefore, it is important not to accept things as they are, particularly now in the age of digitisation.

Technologies have the potential to galvanise action and dilute power (Tsang et al, 2006). They have a sophisticated range to their functionality that can be employed to support or replace traditional assessment methods. They provide ways of developing connections and supporting participation, and offer mediums through which the difficulties that can arouse unnecessary fear can be reduced. The flexible nature of digital tools, and how they can facilitate engagement, pacing and knowledge acquisition provides ample rationale for why they should be, at the very least, explored. We are under no illusion that a book about digital pedagogy is going to change the prescriptive nature of our education system or fully address the discourse around assessment. We are, however, hopeful that embedding technologies, where appropriate, into assessment approaches might lead to a more inclusive student experience – educational encounters that promote engagement and maximise the potential of *every* learner, regardless of their perceived level of ability, or sociological origins. The LearningWheel (Kellsey, 2013) provides an alternative approach, in that assessment is central to its form and function. It is through using methodologies such as this, to establish blended methods, that we have more chance of balancing the dominant diktat that can leave some learners, and indeed teachers, disenfranchised.

CRITICAL **REFLECTION**

It would be useful at this point to pause and to ...

- *list the assessment tools and strategies that you currently use and to consider how these are inclusive and facilitate learning for all students.*

21st-century assessment: The *what*, the *how*, the *why*?

Assessment strategies and assessment processes prior to the introduction of online systems took various forms (Race, 2002). Without going into too much detail, traditionally, they would involve a written task, normally summative in nature, that students would submit to a physical space. The work, usually in hard copy format, would be graded and returned, again physically, to the student group. Learning content delivered against a set of learning outcomes (Race, 2015) most possibly, but not always, were accompanied by formative assignments that would be interspersed throughout teaching events for the purposes of extracting baseline measurements of progression. Technologies, such as the VLE, have changed all of this. Yet the way that assessment methods, as part of the learning process, have emerged has not been without difficulty, for both students and educators alike. Nonetheless, the rapid development of modern technologies and their growing presence in education was deemed reason enough to reimagine the whole notion of assessment (Timmis et al, 2016). However, the resultant reshaping and modification of methods has required educators to begin to think about assessment in what could almost be viewed as radical ways. Since that time, and increasingly so, technologies continue to challenge teaching practices, and assessment is inseparable from this.

The departure from old ways of being to the new continues to stimulate discussion and debate (Pellegrino and Quellmalz, 2010). Nevertheless, what is important is that attention is paid to what or who needs to be assessed, can it or they be assessed, and if so, how, and for what purpose? We have already made the point that any changes to educational processes in the digital age need to be considered systemically, in that attention should be paid to all actors (Fenwick and Edwards, 2010) within a learning network. A learning network, as we see it, includes the learner, learning content, the educator, technologies and the context itself; indeed anything that influences, interacts or is integral to the learning space. Further to an assessment of the digital characteristics of each actor within the network comes the reappraisal of the assessment methods or strategies, to ensure that they are in keeping with the needs of the 21st-century learner and the emerging learning landscape. Neglecting to address part of a learning network can cause the network to fail. Classroom failures are a daily occurrence, and when these occurrences transpire, teachers employ their knowledge, skills and professional resourcefulness to overcome whatever it is that is hindering the effectiveness of the learning space. However, when failure relates to a modern technology, one that requires say, for example, wifi, a piece of software or a device, a very different set of circumstances can arise. It is often said that technologies are great *'when'* they work (Murray, 2016) and indeed they are. Nonetheless, the anxiety and fear that a technological failure can evoke, for example, mid-delivery, could at times be equated to nothing less than a national emergency. Gilbey (2016, np), when writing to newly appointed academic staff, captures this perfectly. He explains that when:

confronted by an urgent need and a large audience ... [computers] can become a truly destructive force – unless you show them who is boss ...

how,

[a] shiny, sophisticated starship console has replaced the elegant teak bench in many institutions, [and how we] now need to attend a course to stand a reasonable chance of successfully driving the functions of the lecture theatre ...

and that,

if someone offers you training, take it ... [or] if all else fails, the standard IT solution of rebooting the entire room will often solve problems of wildly confused settings.

We each have been the 'victims' of tech failure within teaching spaces and appreciate the fear related to this. Hence this is why 21st-century lesson planning in the digital age should include strategies to address these issues, if they occur. Due to the fact that we have engaged with our own digital development, means that we feel much more confident and equipped to manage such situations. This is not to say that there will not be times where a technology failure is beyond our capacity to resolve, but it is reassuring to know that we have an emerging knowledge base and skill set to draw upon.

An increasing amount of resources are being made available to educators that have been designed to appraise each part of the learning network, resources developed with systemic cohesion in mind (JISC, 2015a). But before any adjustments to assessment processes or strategies are made, it is important to return to the issue of digital literacies. Assessment in education begins with the educator, in that an appraisal of digital competence should be undertaken before technologies are incorporated into the practice approach. We introduced you to the work of White (2014) earlier in the book and his *'mapping'* device that was primarily designed to facilitate the charting of digital presence and engagement, in an attempt to evaluate technology usage in education more broadly.

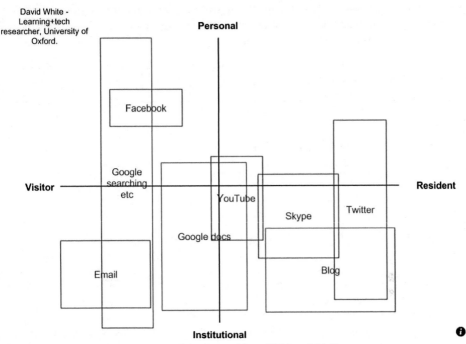

Figure 4.1 Example Visitor and Residents Map (White, 2014).

Example Visitor and Residents Maps www.jisc.ac.uk/guides/evaluating-digital-services/example-visitor-and-resident-maps (White, 2014).

This exercise enables educators not only to map digital presence and engagement but to subsequently analyse digital knowledge and skills for practice so that any digital literacy gaps can be identified and resolved. An appraisal of knowledge and capabilities, in this sense, allows educators to move on from the more technical use of digital resources, which Timmis et al (2016, p 458) explain to be *'limiting the development of more imaginative and creative possibilities'* available. There are a number of other tools that have been developed in this respect. Resources were collated, curated and made available by the Joint Information Systems Committee (JISC) as a result of research that examined technology adoption in education, and which found *'pockets of resistance due to eg lack of confidence, lack of time to engage with new tools, distrust of the academic benefits or cultural attitudes'* (2015a, np) as contributing factors of non-engagement. The links below will take you to these resources. Here you will find a menu of tools that will enable you to further identify digital literacy gaps and methods to address them for practice.

Developing digital literacies: Supporting staff www.jisc.ac.uk/guides/developing-digital-literacies/supporting-staff (JISC, 2015a).

Developing your digital literacies: A range of tools and resources to help you explore your personal digital practices, values and identity

http://jiscdesignstudio.pbworks.com/w/page/60226781/Developing%20your%20digital%20literacies (Beetham, 2014a).

CRITICAL **REFLECTION**

At this point it would be useful to pause and ...

• *spend some time exploring the digital resources made available in the links above and engaging with the Visitor and Residents mapping tool to identify digital literacy gaps and how you might address these.*

Well-designed technology-enhanced assessment offers endless possibilities, for teachers and students. However, as Timmis et al (2016) explain, this requires a shift away from thinking about technology for the purposes of *'efficiency and consistent delivery of assessments ... [to thinking about the] use of technology for rethinking the relationship between learning and assessment'* (p 459). It can provide access to resources and activities that have the capacity to promote and support learner engagement, which in turn can maximise the potential for achievement. This requires thinking about assessment beyond the more traditional methods, through the trialling of approaches like those shared within the LearningWheel VCoP&L (Figure 4.1). Assessing digital knowledge gaps is the first step towards embedding technologies efficiently and effectively into practice. Digital awareness and proficiency is central to this and to assessing, and assisting students to self-assess their own level of digital literacy for learning (JISC, 2015b).

Developing students' digital literacy www.jisc.ac.uk/guides/developing-students-digital-literacy (JISC, 2015a)

All of this is particularly relevant within Initial Teacher Training and the requirement to *'promote the benefits of technology and support learners in its use'* (TETF, 2014, np). Teachers who are engaged with technologies and their own digital development will be more equipped to facilitate the digital development of students, and this is very much required because contrary to popular belief not all students are *'digitally literate'* (Lankshear and Knobel, 2015, p 9). This is also important when thinking about the profile of the student in terms of the assessment of learning needs and access to education.

With regards to the duality of digital development that we spoke about in earlier chapters, the following example drawn from the LearningWheel VCoL&P (Figure 4.1) illustrates how an assessment of trainee teachers' digital knowledge and capabilities led to the development of digital literacies, and the subsequent adoption of blended methods in practice. The

'Trainee Teacher' LearningWheel (Figure 4.1) and an accompanying blog, 'Captaining a LearningWheel' (Davey Nicklin, 2015) evidences not only how being exposed to a range of technologies through engaging with the model facilitated digital development, as per professional requirements, but also how it alleviated practice concerns. The following comments, taken from interviews with the student teachers, authenticate the impact of the LearningWheel model when employed purposively by a digitally equipped educator:

What I learned from incorporating these learning technologies into my lessons is that students do appreciate breaks from the norm, and I believe that if you can get students to learn without them realising it, then that is a great thing.

Stephanie Sekula (cited in Davey Nicklin, 2015, np)

During my teaching practice I was worried about how I could make effective use of technology within my teaching practice.

Laura-May Tovey (cited in Davey Nicklin, 2015, np)

The curated spokes of this wheel contain a wide selection of digital resources employed by educators for assessment purposes – contributions that evidence the *what*, the *how*, and the *why* of the model. For example, as you can see, SurveyMonkey was used to create a quiz that facilitated formative assessment, while Video was employed as a means of recording content for peer and tutor review and Wordpress was utilised due to features that permit collating and curating content for assessment revision. The way these digital resources have been used evidence the flexibility and the creativity that is made available through technology-enhanced and blended approaches to assessment. Further to this, Davey's (2015, np) use of the model shows how collaboration on a wider scale can provide access to the knowledge that exists within a global *'community of practice'* (Wenger, 2000). The CoActEd learner mapping tool (Taylor and Kellsey, 2016) was developed with this in mind, in that it aims to proactively engage students in a reflective task that can enable them to assess knowledge and build upon their professional network.

Figure 4.2 Trainee Teacher LearningWheel (Kellsey, 2016a).

Trainee Teacher LearningWheel http://learningwheel.co.uk/2016/05/trainee-teacher/ (Kellsey, 2016a).

The LearningWheel website (Kellsey, 2016a) offers many more tried and tested methods of using technologies for the purposes of assessment for learning (Hargreaves et al, 2014), as opposed to assessment of learning (Harlen, 2007). Such technologies support formative and summative assessment strategies and methods in a manner that is engaging, flexible and paced. The informed use of technologies to strengthen and reinforce assessment methods can trigger self-assessment, peer assessment and provide academic assessment that is conveyed incrementally, therefore providing time to absorb and act upon the feedback received.

CRITICAL **REFLECTION**

At this point again it would be useful to pause and think about ...

- *the ways in which you assess a student's digital literacy and the methods you use to facilitate assessment of learning in a digital respect.*

All of this being said, without adequate infrastructure and institutional support digital development is difficult to access and progress. The links below will again take you to resources that will enable you to think about the educational environment as part of the learning network, so as to identify any barriers there might be to fully engaging with the range of technologies available, those pertinent to assessment for learning. The first is again from Beetham (2014b) who has collated a number of examples and solutions, with the second from Gray (2016) more specific to assessment, illustrating how the institution and environment are significant to the ability of educators to develop.

Developing digitally literate Institutions http://jiscdesignstudio.pbworks.com/w/page/60226492/Developing%20digitally%20literate%20institutions (Beetham, 2014b).

Electronic management of assessment (EMA) in higher education: Processes and systems www.jisc.ac.uk/guides/electronic-management-of-assessment-processes-and-systems (Gray, 2016).

We have discussed the assessment of the various actors within the learning network and provided resources that will assist in considering the digital development of each. Here, again, we offer readers an opportunity to interact with the LearningWheel model through contributing spoke suggestions (Figure 1.2) to the assessment mode of the 'LearningWheel Book: Top Apps and Resources' (Kellsey and Taylor, 2016, np). Using *what*, *why* and *how* as prompts, readers are encouraged to provide practice examples (Figure 1.2) that employ a digital resource to support assessment for learning.

LearningWheel Book: Top Apps and Resources

https://docs.google.com/spreadsheets/d/1EDRN4UaR6m93B_YEMGTZ8EOIS
IWnfWsENkcDByWtWIM/edit#gid=2134954465 (Kellsey and Taylor, 2016, np).

We began this chapter by reviewing the issues with assessment as we see them, before moving on to think about how any changes to assessment strategies need to start with an assessment of each actor within a learning network. We considered how technologies can, have and are shaping assessment methods in practice and drew upon examples from the LearningWheel VCoL&P to illustrate how this is possible and to what effect. The LearningWheel came about as a result of an initial 'assessment' of digital resources pertinent to developing teaching practice. It grew into a four-dimensional 'assessment' model for 'assessing' technology-enhanced teaching methods and blended approaches. True to its 'assessment' origins it continues to call for contributions that have been 'assessed' as improving practice and above all the student experience. Collaborators to the LearningWheel VCoL&P are prepared to take risks with assessment, in that they are willing to reconsider their methods in attempts to address notions of, *'fairness, reliability and validity'* (McDowell, 1995, p 311). They exploit technologies, and work with the fear of letting go of what would be traditionally thought of as safe methods because they understand that staying safe reduces the possibility of creating a *'level playing field'* (McDowell, 1995, p 302). As Sparkes, in a classic romantic novel says, *'nothing that is worthwhile is ever easy ... remember that'* (1998, p 131). Viewing assessment as ongoing, incremental and affective (Race et al, 2005) will be significant to how we embed technologies into assessment approaches, that is if we are to be effective in this respect.

REFERENCES

Astin, A W (2012) *Assessment for Excellence: The Philosophy and Practice of Assessment and Evaluation in Higher Education*. New York: Rowman & Littlefield Publishers.

Beetham, H (2014a) Developing your digital literacies: A range of tools and resources to help you explore your personal digital practices, values and identity. [online] Available at: http://jiscdesignstudio.pbworks.com/w/page/60226781/Developing%20your%20digital%20literacies (accessed 25 September 2016).

Beetham, H (2014b) Developing digitally literate institutions. [online] Available at: http://jiscdesignstudio.pbworks.com/w/page/60226492/Developing%20digitally%20literate%20institutions (accessed 25 September 2016).

Boud, D (1995) Assessment and Learning: Contradictory or Complementary?, in Knight, P (ed) *Assessment for Learning in Higher Education*, pp 35–48. London: Kogan.

Boud, D (2013) *Enhancing Learning through Self-assessment*. London: Routledge.

Boud, D and Molloy, E (2013) What is the Problem with Feedback?, in Boud, D and Molloy, E (eds) *Feedback in Higher and Professional Education: Understanding It and Doing It Well*, pp 1–10. Abingdon, Oxon: Routledge.

Court, K (2014) Tutor Feedback on Draft Essays: Developing Students' Academic Writing and Subject Knowledge. *Journal of Further and Higher Education*, 38(3): 327–45.

Davey Nicklin, K (2015) Captaining a LearningWheel [blog]. [online] Available at: http://learningwheel.co.uk/ 2016/05/trainee-teacher/ (accessed 25 September 2016).

Dorling, D (2014) Is the British Education System Designed to Polarise People? *The Guardian*. [online] Available at: www.theguardian.com/education/2014/feb/04/education-system-polarises-people-economic-inequality (accessed 23 September 2016).

Falchikov, N (2013) *Improving Assessment through Student Involvement: Practical Solutions for Aiding Learning in Higher and Further Education*. London: Routledge.

Fenwick, T and Edwards, R (2010) *Actor-Network Theory in Education*. Abingdon, Oxon: Routledge.

Froggett, L (2002) *Love, Hate and Welfare: Psychosocial Approaches to Policy and Practice*. Bristol: The Policy Press.

Gibbs, G (1999) Using Assessment Strategically to Change the Way Students Learn, in Brown, S and Glasner, A (eds) *Assessment Matters in Higher Education*, pp 41–53. Buckingham: Open University Press.

Gilbey, J (2016) Seven essential tips for surviving the new academic year. *The Times Higher Education (THE)*. [online] Available at: www.timeshighereducation.com/features/seven-essential-tips-for-surviving-the-new-academic-year (accessed 1 October 2016).

Goodwin, A L (ed) (2012) *Assessment for Equity and Inclusion: Embracing All Our Children*. London: Routledge.

Gray, L (2016) Electronic Management of Assessment (EMA) in Higher Education: Processes and Systems. [online] Available at: www.jisc.ac.uk/guides/electronic-management-of-assessment-processes-and-systems (accessed 28 September 2016).

Harlen, W (2007) *Assessment of Learning*. London: Sage.

Harris, K K (2015) An examination of the relationship of course evaluations to student retention and student success in the community college online classroom [thesis]. [online] Available at: http://gradworks.umi.com/ 37/37/3737176.html (accessed 4 October 2016).

Ingram, N and Waller, R (2016) Higher education and the reproduction of social elites. *Discover Society*. [online] Available at: http://discoversociety.org/2015/05/05/higher-education-and-the-reproduction-of-social-elites/?utm_content=buffer7e451&utm_medium=social&utm_source=twitter.com&utm_campaign=buffer (accessed 3 October 2016).

JISC (2015a) Supporting staff. [online] Available at: www.jisc.ac.uk/guides/developing-digital-literacies/ supporting-staff (accessed 24 September 2016).

JISC (2015b) Developing students' digital literacy. [online] Available at: www.jisc.ac.uk/guides/developing-students-digital-literacy (accessed 24 September 2016).

Kellsey, D (2013) LearningWheel: A model of digital pedagogy. [online] Available at: http://learningwheel. co.uk/about-the-learning-wheel/model-digital-pedagogy/ (accessed 14 September 2016).

Kellsey, D (2016a) Trainee Teacher LearningWheel. [online] Available at: http://learningwheel.co.uk/2016/05/ trainee-teacher/ (accessed 25 September 2016).

Kellsey, D (2016b) Assistive Technology LearningWheel. [online] Available at: http://learningwheel. co.uk/2016/06/assistivetech-twitter/ (accessed 25 September 2016).

Kellsey, D and Taylor, A M L (2016) LearningWheel Book: Top Apps and Resources. [online] Available at: https://docs.google.com/spreadsheets/d/1EDRN4UaR6m93B_YEMGTZ8EOISIWnfWsENkcDByWtWIM/ edit#gid=2134954465 (accessed 30 September 2016).

Kirkwood, A and Price, L (2008). Assessment and Student Learning: A Fundamental Relationship and the Role of Information and Communication Technologies. *Open Learning*, 23(1): 5–16.

Lankshear, C and Knobel, M (2015) Digital Literacy and Digital Literacies: Policy, Pedagogy and Research Considerations for Education. *Nordic Journal of Digital Literacy*, 9: 8–20.

McDowell, L (1995) The Impact of Innovative Assessment on Student Learning. *Programmed Learning*, 32,(4): 302–13.

Meyer, J and Land, R (2006) *Overcoming Barriers to Student Understanding: Threshold Concepts and Troublesome Knowledge*. Abingdon, Oxon: Routledge.

Murray, J (2016) Technology in the classroom: What happens when it fails? [blog]. [online] Available at: www.teachhub.com/technology-classroom-what-happens-when-it-failsAMLT (accessed 26 September 2016).

Orsmond, P, Merry, S and Reiling, K (2005) Biology Students' Utilization of Tutors' Formative Feedback: A Qualitative Interview Study. *Assessment & Evaluation in Higher Education*, 30(4): 369–86.

Pellegrino, J W and Quellmalz, E S (2010) Perspectives on the Integration of Technology and Assessment. *Journal of Research on Technology in Education*, 43(2): 119–34.

Race, P (2002) Why fix assessment? A discussion paper. [online] Available at: www.sddu.leeds.ac.uk/online_resources/phil%20assess.htm (accessed 23 September 2016).

Race, P (2014) *The Lecturer's Toolkit: A Practical Guide to Assessment, Learning and Teaching*. Oxon, Routledge.

Race, P (2015) *The Lecturer's Toolkit*. 4th ed. London: Routledge.

Race, P, Brown, S and Smith, B (2005) *500 Tips on Assessment*. 2nd ed. London: Routledge.

Rowntree, D (1987) *Assessing Students: How Shall We Know Them?* London: Harper & Row.

Schmeck, R R (1988) An Introduction to Strategies and Styles of Learning. *Learning Strategies and Learning Styles*, pp 3–19. New York: Springer.

Sparkes, N (1998) *Message in a Bottle: Do You Believe in Love?* London: Little Brown Book Company.

Taras, M (2005) Assessment – Summative and Formative – Some Theoretical Reflections. *British Journal of Educational Studies*, 53(4): 466–78.

Taylor, A M L and Kellsey, D (2016) The CoActED learner maps. [online] Available at: http://learningwheel.co.uk/call-coacted-learner-maps/ (accessed 30 September 2016).

The Education and Training Foundation (TETF) (2014) Professional Standards for Teachers and Trainers – England. [online] Available at: www.et-foundation.co.uk/supporting/support-practitioners/professional-standards/ (accessed 23 September 2016).

Timmis, S, Broadfoot, P, Sutherland, R and Oldfield, A (2016) Rethinking Assessment in a Digital Age: Opportunities, Challenges and Risks. *British Education Research Journal*, 42: 454–76.

Tsang, P, Kwan, R and Fox, R (2006) *Enhancing Learning Through Technology*. River Edge, NJ: WSPC.

Weaver, M R (2006) Do Students Value Feedback? Student Perceptions of Tutors' Written Responses. *Assessment & Evaluation in Higher Education*, 31(3): 379–94.

Wenger, E (2000) *Communities of Practice: Learning, Meaning, and Identity*. Cambridge: Cambridge University Press.

White, D (2014) Example visitor and resident maps. *JISC Evaluating Digital Services*. [online] Available at: www.jisc.ac.uk/guides/evaluating-digital-services/example-visitor-and-resident-maps (accessed 7 June 2016).

The LearningWheel: A labour of love!

This book has provided an insight into the LearningWheel model and outlined how it can be used to critique and develop digital literacies for the creation of contemporary learning experiences. It has offered a summary of each of the modes of engagement, and illustrated their application in practice through examples taken from the LearningWheel VCoP&L. Woven throughout the chapters are a number of critical reflections, positioned at junctures where we felt it would be most useful to stop and pause for thought. In addition to these learning opportunities, we have incorporated into the text interactive links aimed at enabling educators to engage, in a very real sense, with their own digital development. An ongoing evaluation of the LearningWheel methodology has evidenced how experiential learning such as this can provide educators with the confidence required to promote and support digital development within their respective institutions and more importantly, within their student groups. We have discussed the way in which the model has emerged and have drawn your attention to the different types of wheels that are now available for usage across the vast array of subject areas that make up the teaching and learning community (Figure 5.1).

Types of LearningWheels

RESOURCE
LEARNINGWHEEL

Targeted digital
resources.

Resource Wheels are detailed practical guides with numerous spokes signposting to key resources such as Moodle, Blendspace by TES, Twitter and QR codes introducing the wide range of opportunities available within each of those applications.

SUBJECT SPECIFIC
LEARNINGWHEEL

Mapping digital resources
to specific subject,
modules/units.

Subject Specific LearningWheels are designed to offer practical ways in which a teacher can use a digital resources e.g.Twitter, Blendspace etc.within their specialist subject area, e.g. English language, Maths, Radiotherapy, Education Studies, Hairdressing.

CONFERENCE
LEARNINGWHEEL

Captures technology usage
Within a particular
learning community.

The Conference LearningWheel design builds upon the original LearningWheel model in that it aims to capture technology usage within a particular community of learning or practice, whilst sharing the collated and curated content more widely throughout the community in question.

MORE
LEARNING
WHEELS
TO FOLLOW

Learn more on Twitter...
#LEARNINGWHEEL
@DebKellsey @LearningWheel

Figure 5.1 Types of LearningWheels (Kellsey, 2016).

Types of LearningWheels https://drive.google.com/drive/u/0/folders/0B8EjX-Oze LTaQUtSU0p3UFppVkk (Kellsey, 2016).

Throughout the text are references to the unprecedented way in which technologies are shaping the world and our experience of it. We have noted the time lag between technology inception and adoption and have spoken of the dangers of this continuing. Attention has been paid to the copious claims that have been made about technologies, over the years, that have resulted in a cautiousness about their usage in practice. This kind of speculation and the associated predictions have generated an unnecessary angst that has led to a disconnect between teaching methods and what is going on in the wider world.

This poem by an anonymous teacher captures perfectly what we mean:

> *'Antiquated'*
> *Mr. Edison says*
> *That the radio will supplant the teacher.*
> *Already one may learn languages by means of Victrola records.*
> *The moving picture will visualize*
> *What the radio fails to get across.*
> *Teachers will be relegated to the backwoods,*
> *With fire-horses,*
> *And long-haired women;*
> *Or, perhaps shown in museums.*
> *Education will become a matter*
> *Of pressing the button.*
> *Perhaps I can get a position at the switchboard.*

(Anonymous Teacher, 1920, cited in Cuban, 1986, pp 4–5)

Even though this poem was penned significantly earlier than the current provocative discourse used to explain digitalisation, such as explosion (Henriksen et al, 2016) or revolution (Collins and Halverson, 2010), it characterises the impact of language and its historic role in shaping perceptions about that which is new, unfamiliar or unknown. Inasmuch as it might feel easier to remain with the old ... unless we take a hold of the new, it has the potential, more than we realise, to take a hold of us (Susskind and Susskind, 2015). And this is not to say that we buy into the age old adage, *'man ... [or more appropriately, human] versus machine'* (Davenport and Kirby, 2016, p 2), but we just want to restate how important it is to stay alert to the role of technology in shaping the debate. This requires us to move away from stories that describe how it was, and to move towards a more forward-looking narrative which reflects how it is or indeed how it could be. The marked progression in the use of technologies to support or replace traditional methods and approaches across the teaching and learning community cannot be denied. However, casting our minds back to the Dearing Report (1997, p 202) that explained how:

the innovative exploitation of Communications and Information Technology (C&IT) holds out much promise for improving the quality, flexibility and effectiveness of higher education. The potential benefits will extend to, and affect the practice of, learning and teaching and research.

This leads us to question how far we have come and where we are now.

For us, engagement with the LearningWheel model and its growing VCoL&P provides a vehicle through which the *'potential benefits'* of technologies in education can be realised (Dearing, 1997, p 202), in that it demonstrates what can happen when educators take the leap into the digital world and all that it has to offer. There is no denying, for any of us, that technologies can and will pose a different set of problems for education and educators as they emerge – issues such as ethics, online safety, professionalism and most likely a whole host of other unimagined challenges that have yet to arise. All this aside, and to recap, 21st-century learners need 21st-century learning experiences, shaped by 21st-century teachers in 21st-century learning environments. Working through all this may be *'troublesome'* (Meyer and Land, 2006) but as we said in Chapter 4 it will be *'worth it'* (Sparkes, 1998).

In drawing the book to a close we would like to take this opportunity to explain why we decided that 'The LearningWheel: A labour of love' was a fitting note on which to end. The LearningWheel is a project that has been nearly five years in the making. Throughout the early stages of its inception there were many more non-believers than believers, and there are those who, even today, remain unconvinced. It has taken a significant amount of time and energy to convince, what is now a large percentage of the global teaching and learning population of its pedagogic value, but for those now engaged it has become something that we can only describe as a labour of love. We have and do spend an incredible amount of time nurturing it, maintaining it, and at times, containing it. At the time of writing we are in the process of developing the LearningWheel Research Hub and a LearningWheel app that will make it even more accessible than it currently is. The more people that get involved, the more there is to do, but it is this that maintains our commitment to it and the VCoL&P that is being forged through it. We set out hoping that this book would be, at the very least, aspirational, in that we aspired to empower, and to promote achievable change. However, now we have got to the end we wonder if, for any of you, it has been what Laurillard (2007, cited in Beetham and Sharpe, 2007, xv) considers to be *'transformational'*. So on that note here is our final critical reflection …

CRITICAL **REFLECTION**

As it is the last time that we will pause together 'in this space' we would ask that …

- *you use the hashtag #learningwheel to send us, @DebKellsey and @amltaylor66, a tweet to let us know if you have found the book 'aspirational, troublesome, or indeed transformational'.*

REFERENCES

Beetham, H and Sharpe R (2007) *Rethinking Pedagogy for a Digital Age: Designing and Delivering E-learning*. London: Routledge.

Collins, A and Halverson, R (2010) The Second Educational Revolution: Rethinking Education in the Age of Technology. *Journal of Computer Assisted Learning*, 26(1): 18–27.

Cuban, L (1986) *Teachers and Machines: The Classroom Use of Technologies since 1920*. New York: Teachers College Press.

Davenport, T H and Kirby, J (2016) *Only Humans Need Apply: Winners and Losers in the Age of Smart Machines*. London: Harper Collins Publishers.

Dearing, R (1997) *The Dearing Report. The National Committee of Enquiry into Higher Education*. London: HMSO.

Henriksen, D, Mishra, P and Fisser, P (2016) Infusing Creativity and Technology in 21st Century Education: A Systemic View for Change. *Journal of Educational Technology & Society*, 19(3): 27–37.

Kellsey, D (2016) Types of LearningWheels. [online] Available at: https://drive.google.com/drive/u/0/folders/0B8EjX-OzeLTaQUtSU0p3UFppVkk (accessed 18 September 2016).

Laurillard, D (2007) Preface, in Beetham, H and Sharpe, R (2013) (eds) *Rethinking Pedagogy for a Digital Age: Designing and Delivering E-Learning*, pp xix–xxi. London: Routledge.

Meyer, J and Land, R (2006) *Overcoming Barriers to Student Understanding: Threshold Concepts and Troublesome Knowledge*. Abingdon, Oxon: Routledge.

Sparkes, N (1998) *Message in a Bottle: Do You Believe in Love?* London: Little Brown Book Company.

Susskind, R E and Susskind, D (2015) *The Future of the Professions: How Technology will Transform the Work of Human Experts*. Oxford: Open University Press.

INDEX